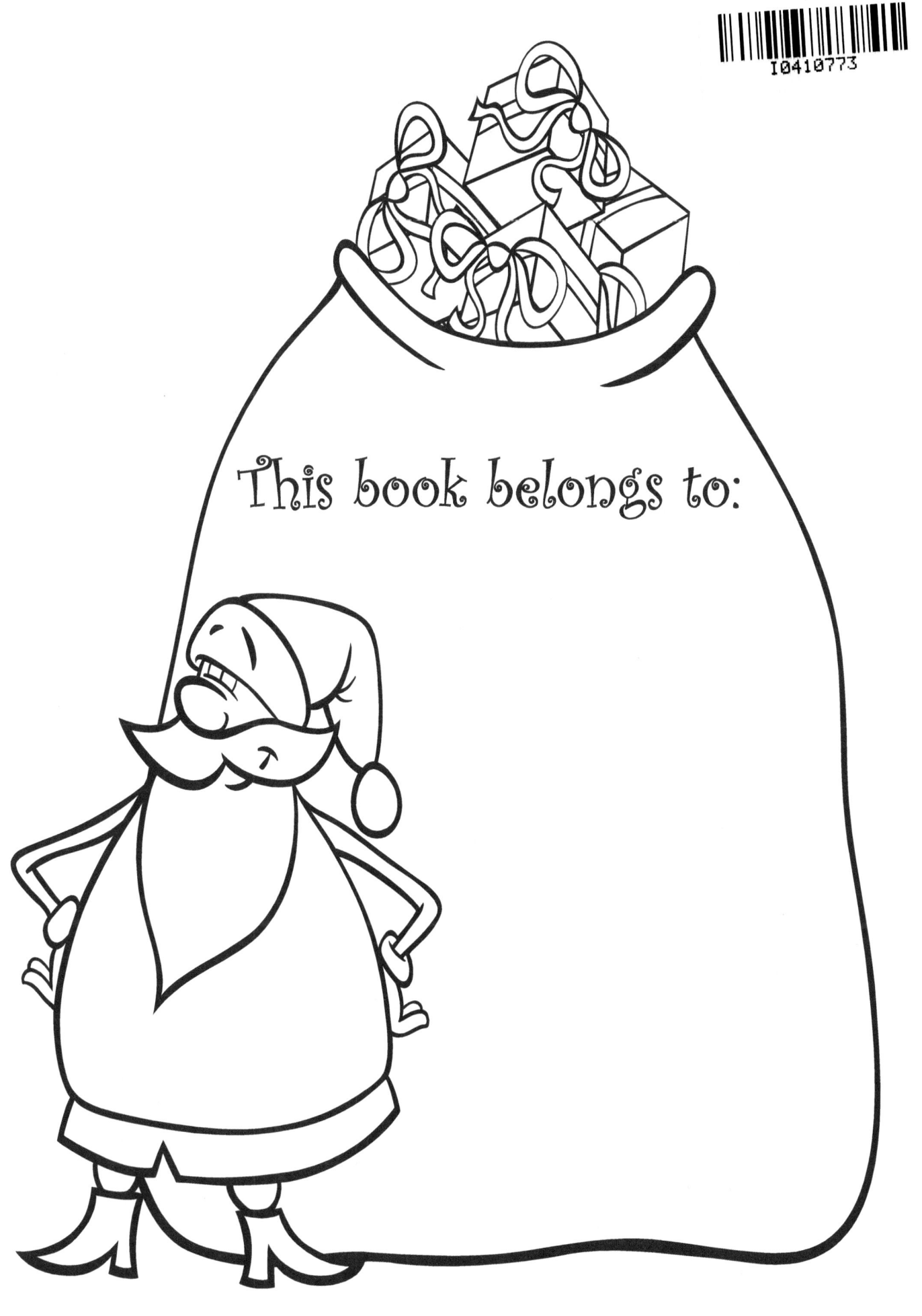

This book belongs to:

Silly Santa, Silly Elves!

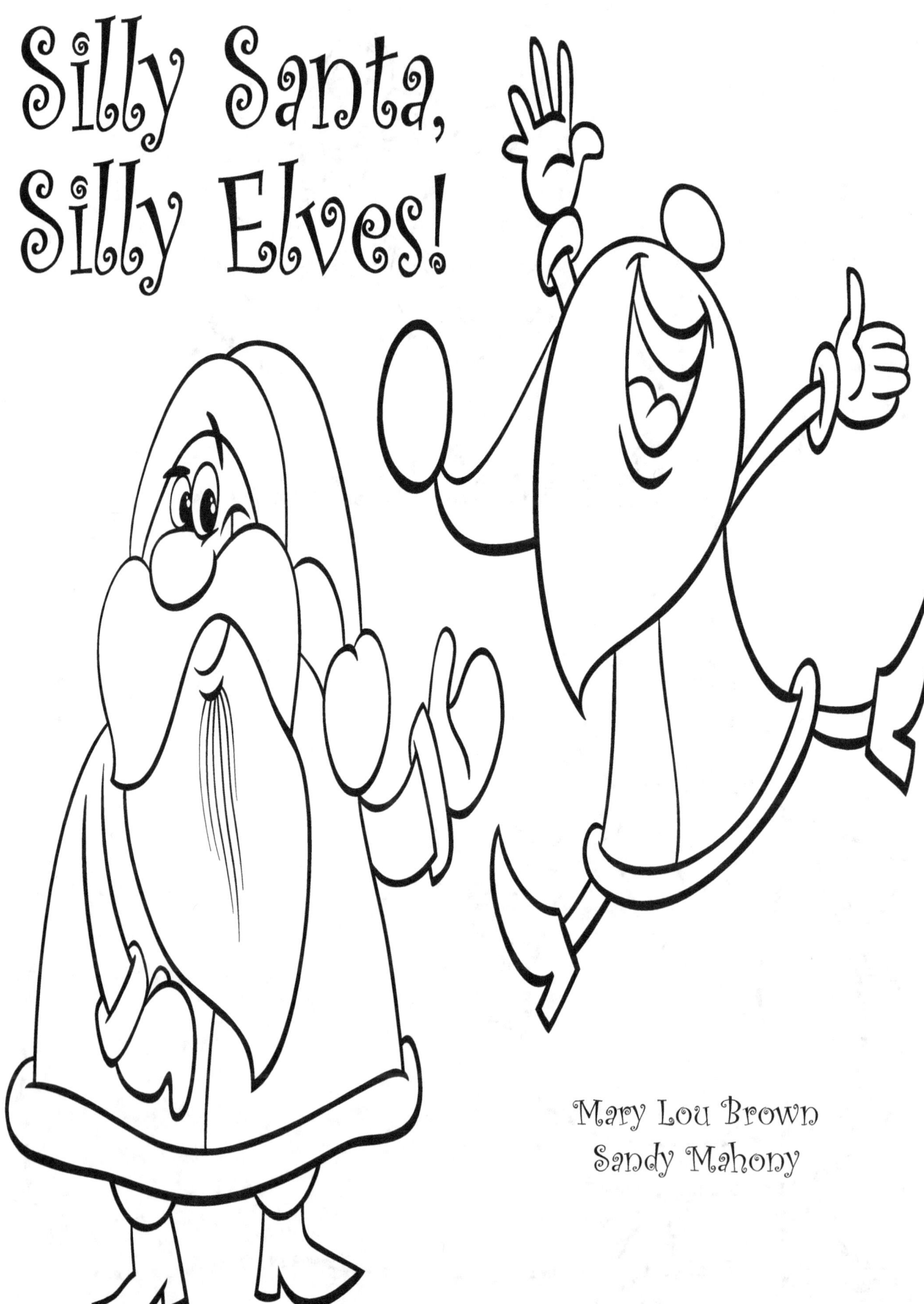

Mary Lou Brown
Sandy Mahony

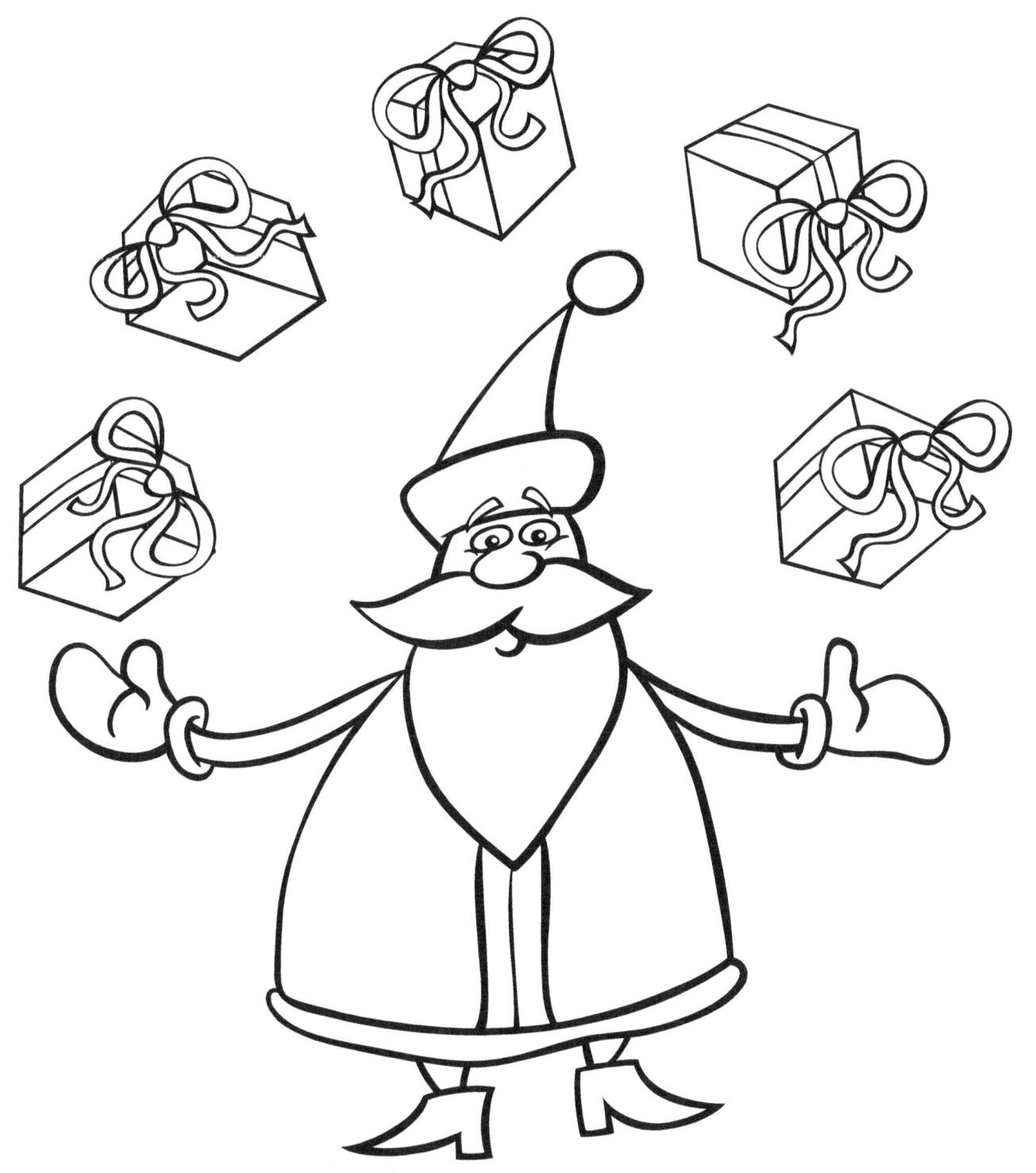

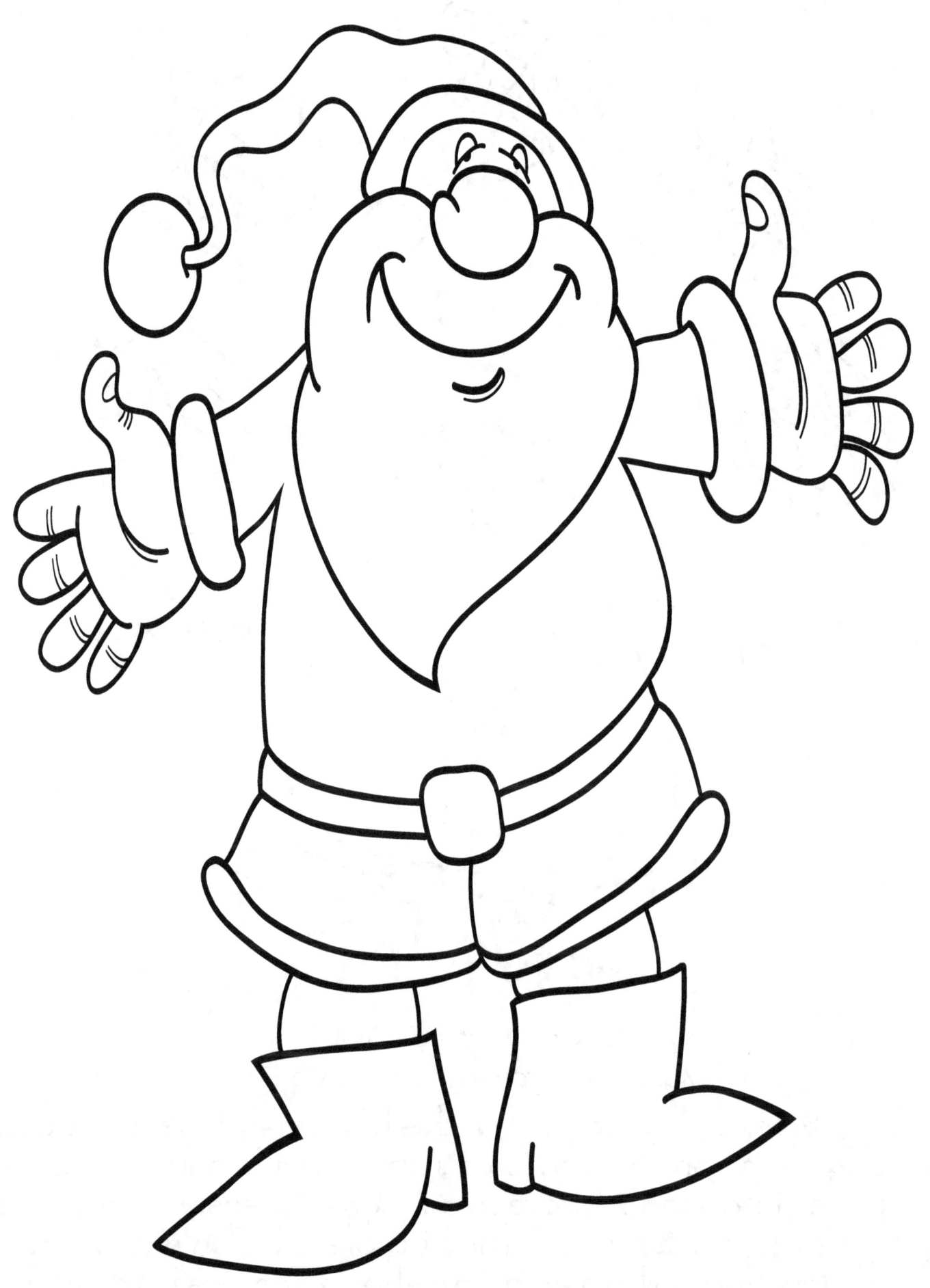

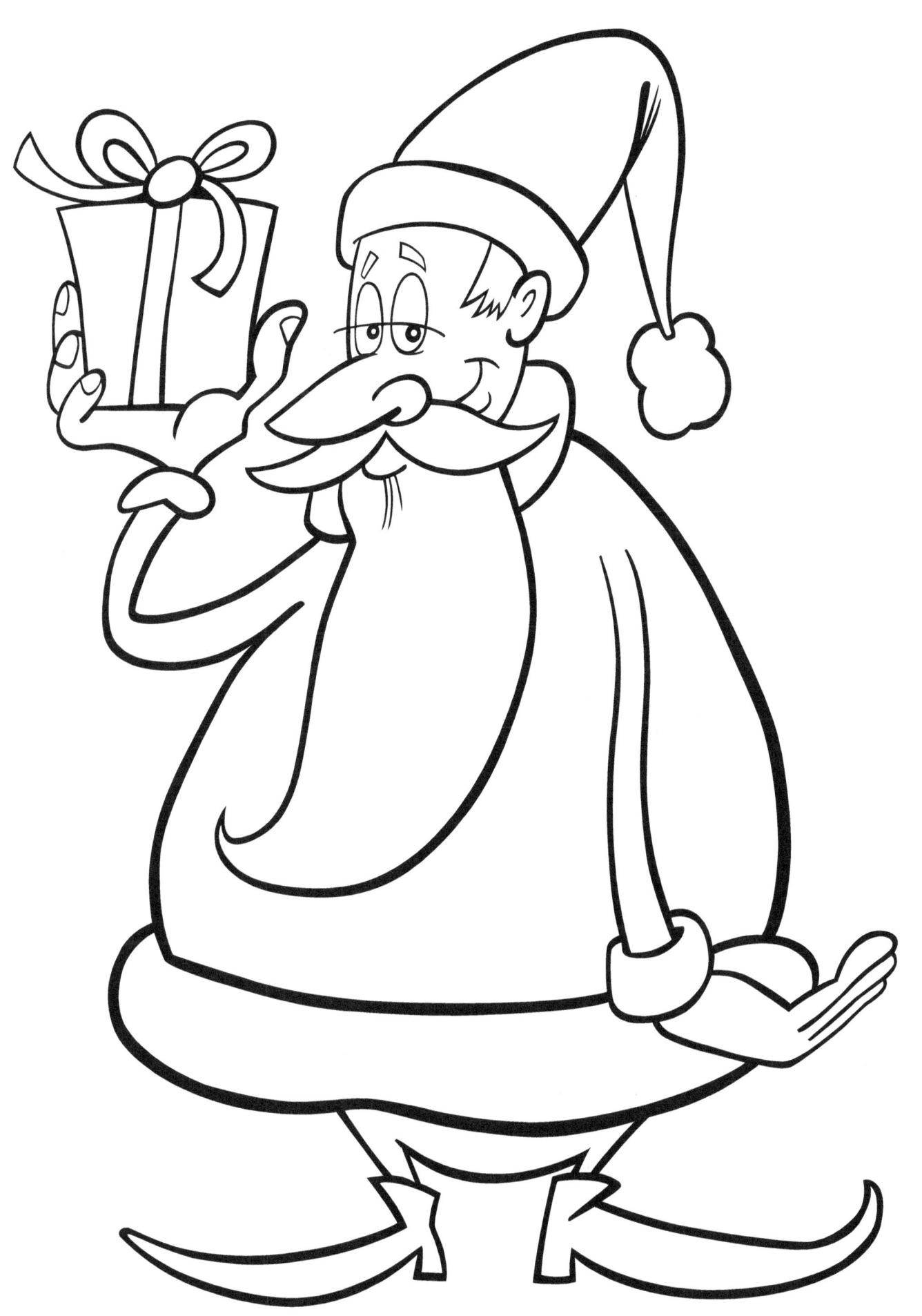

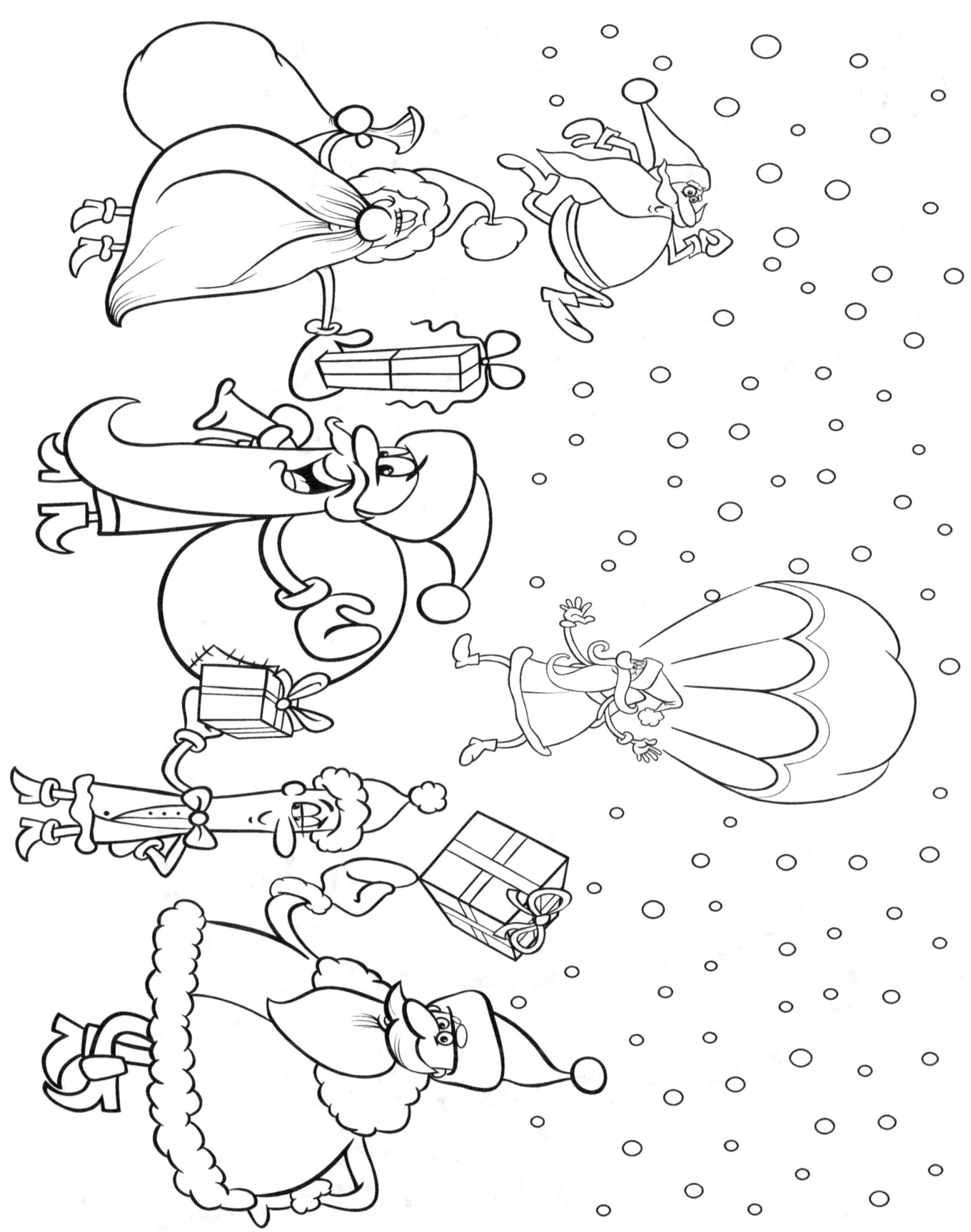

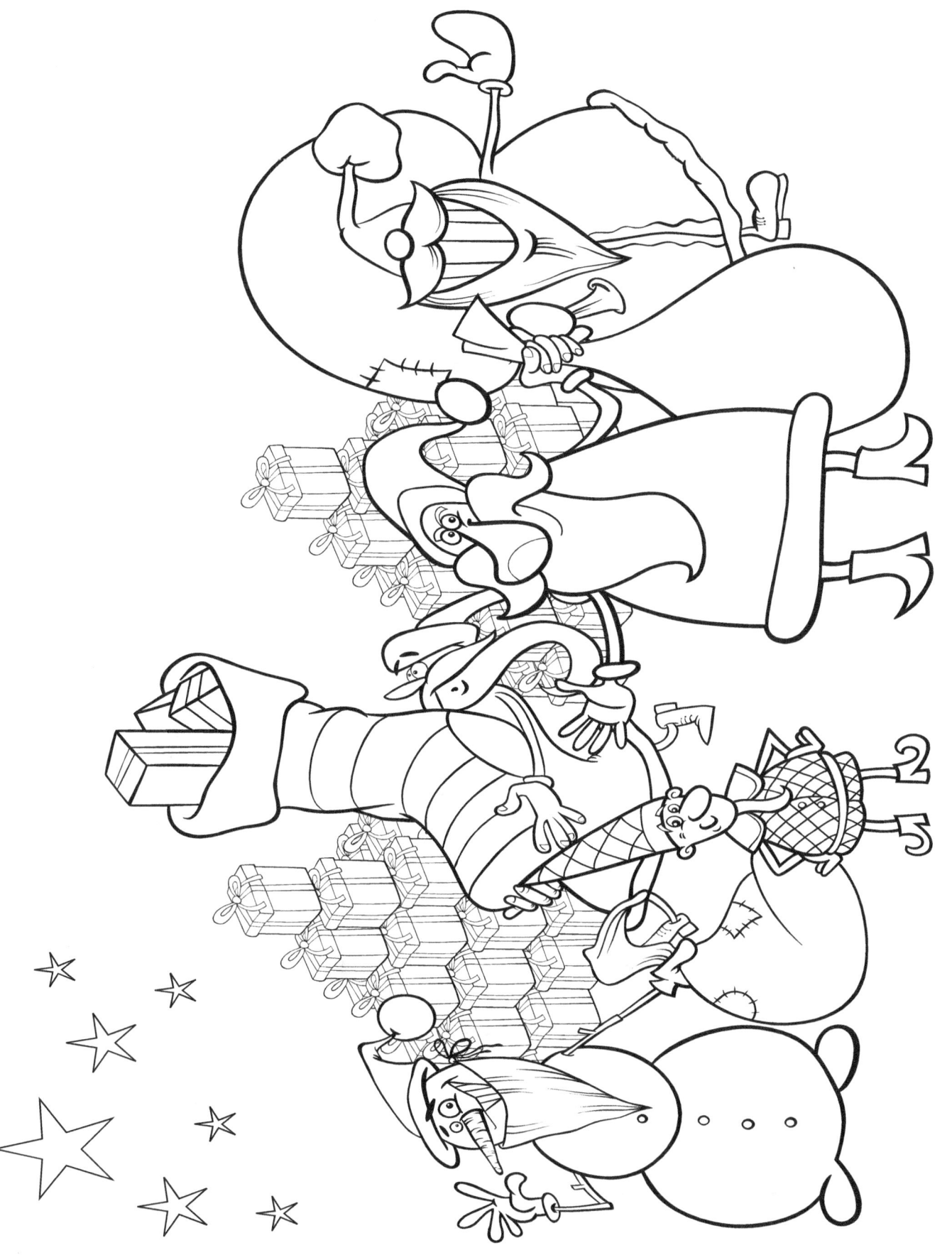

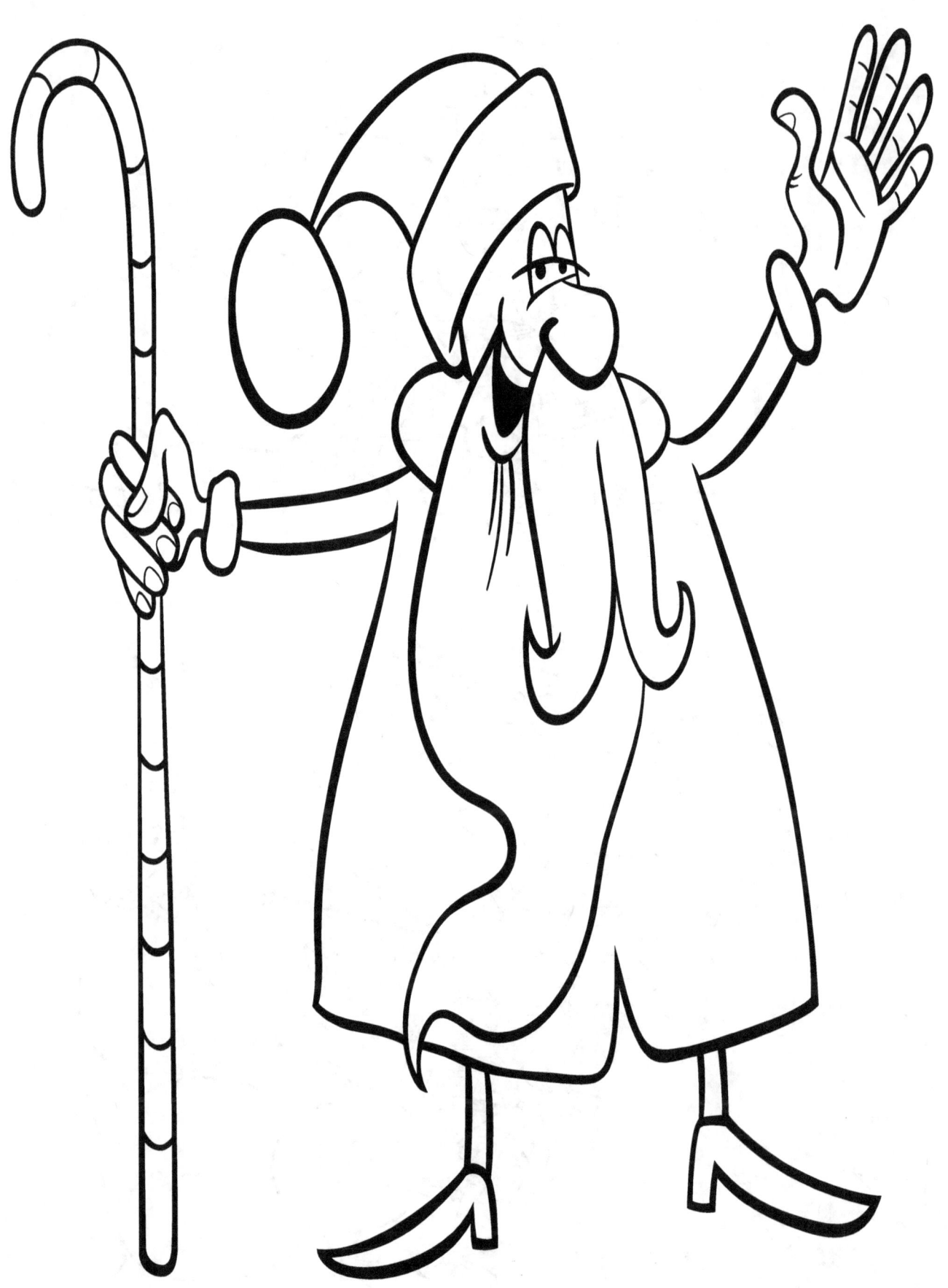

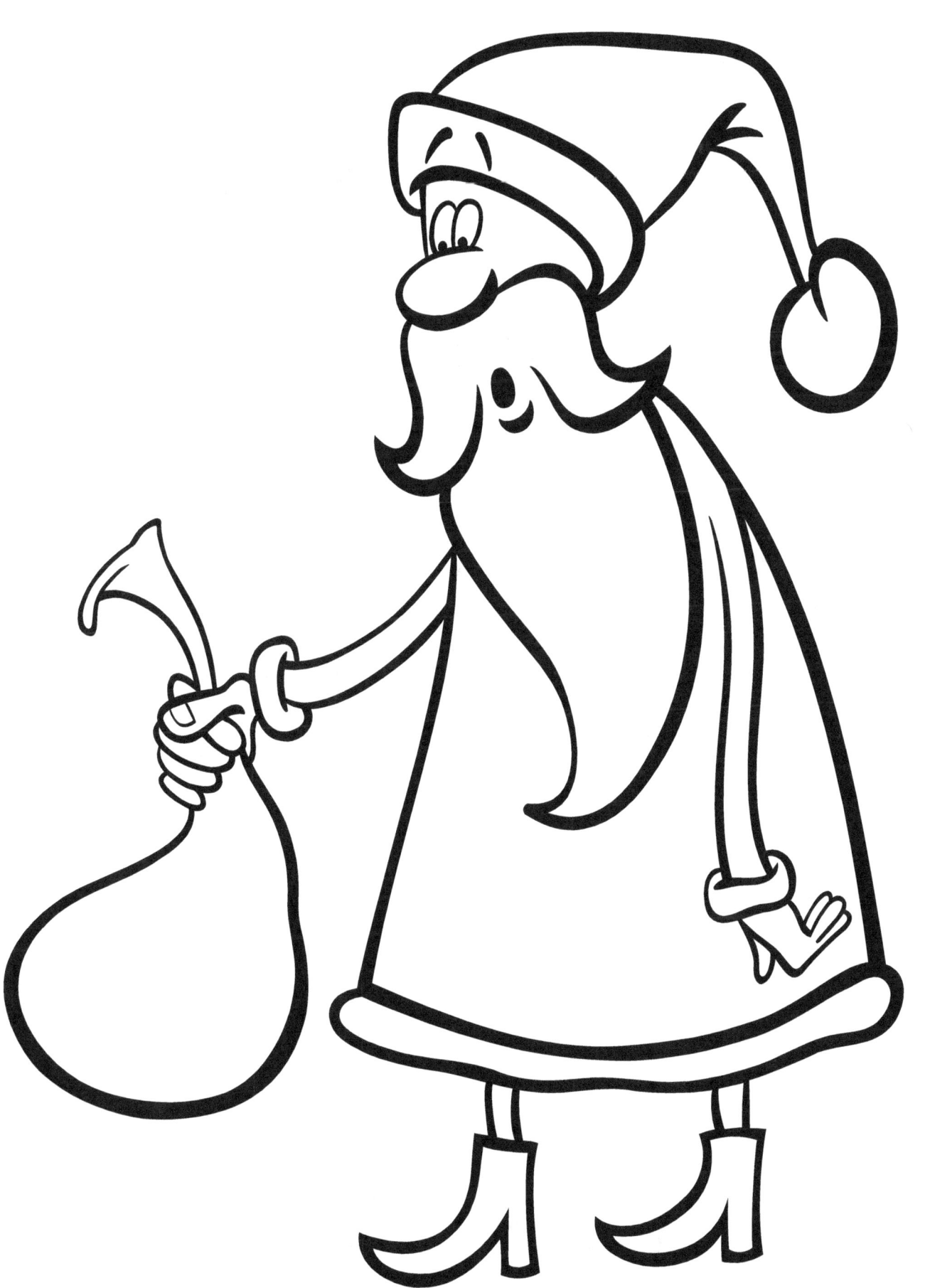

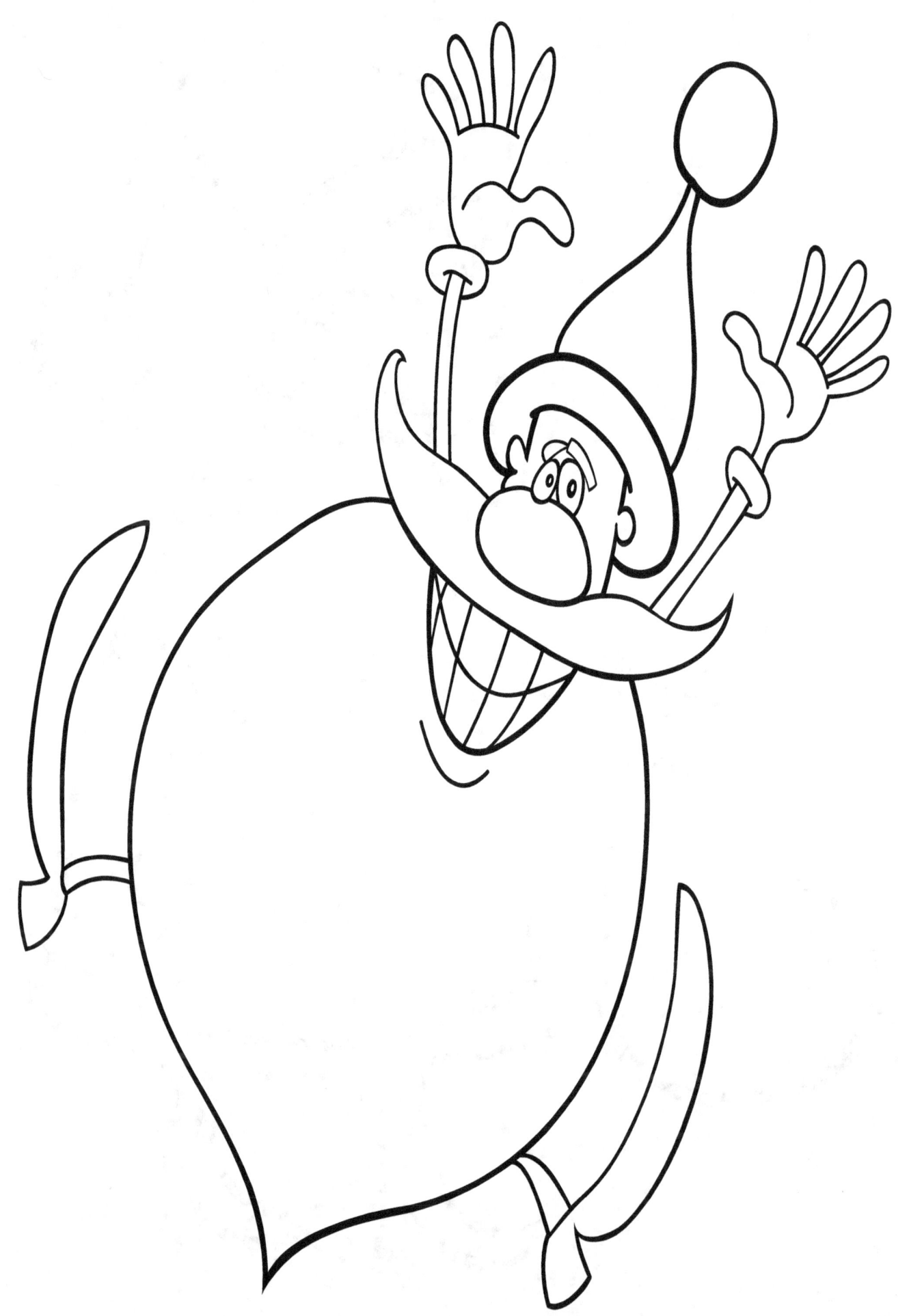

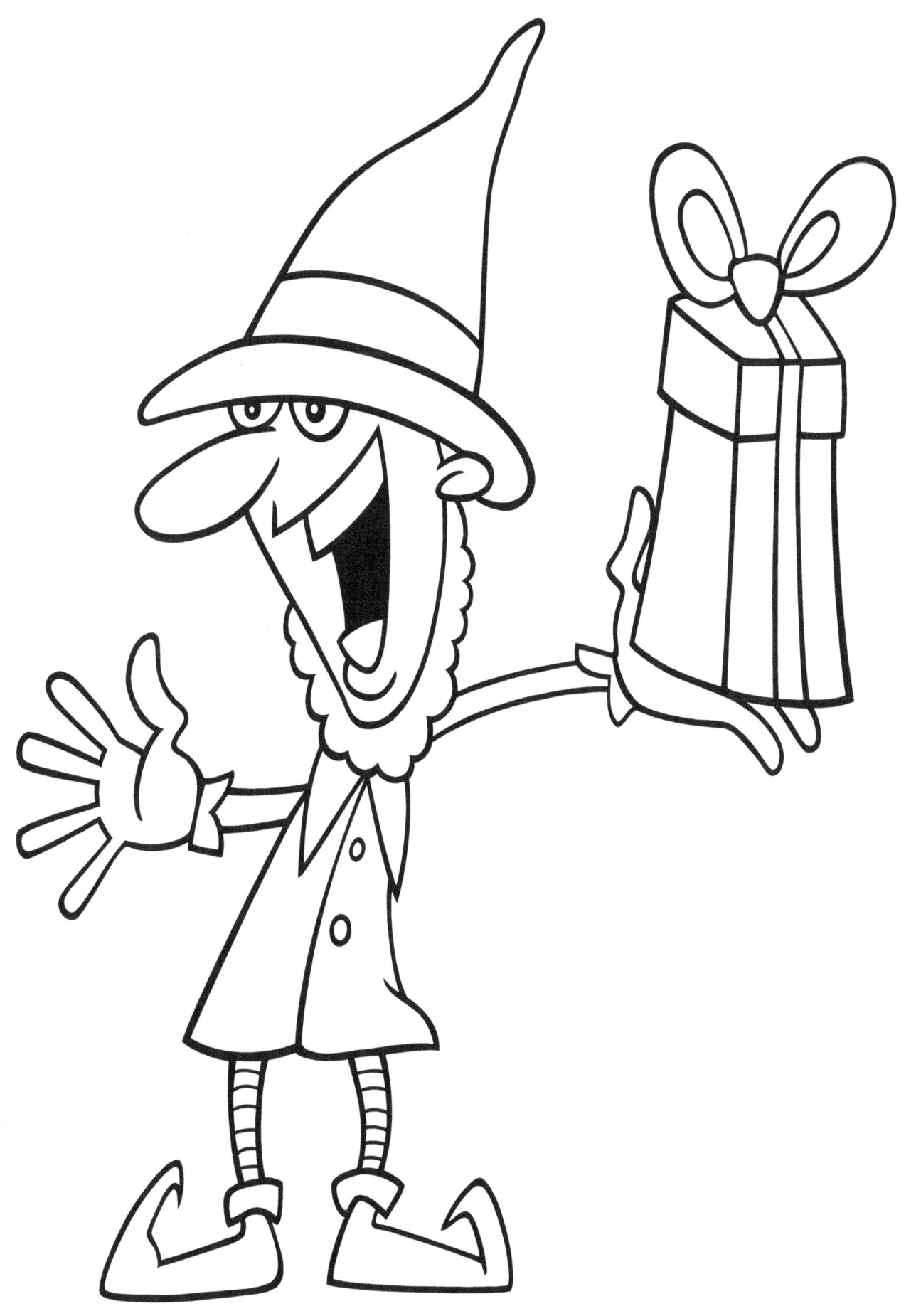

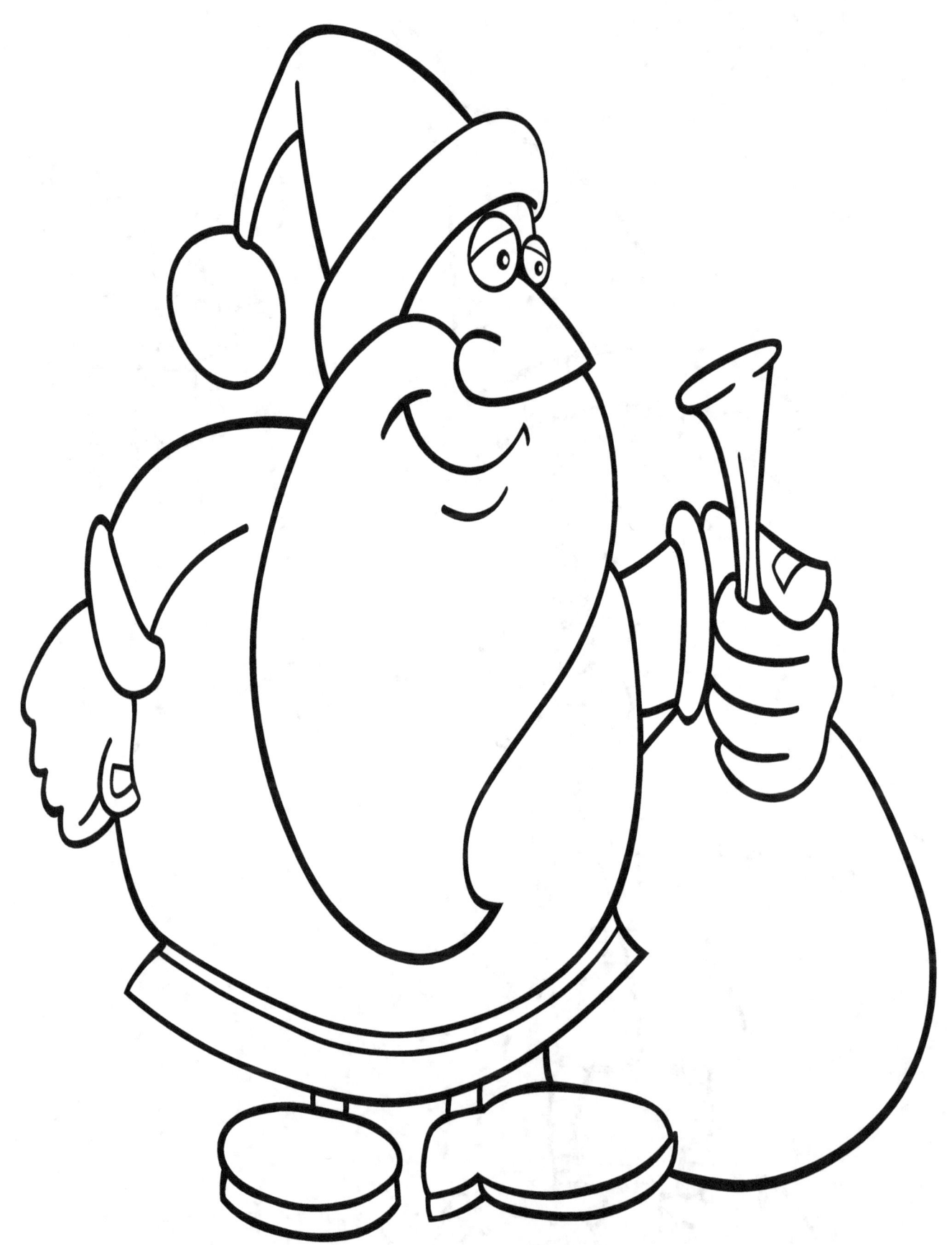

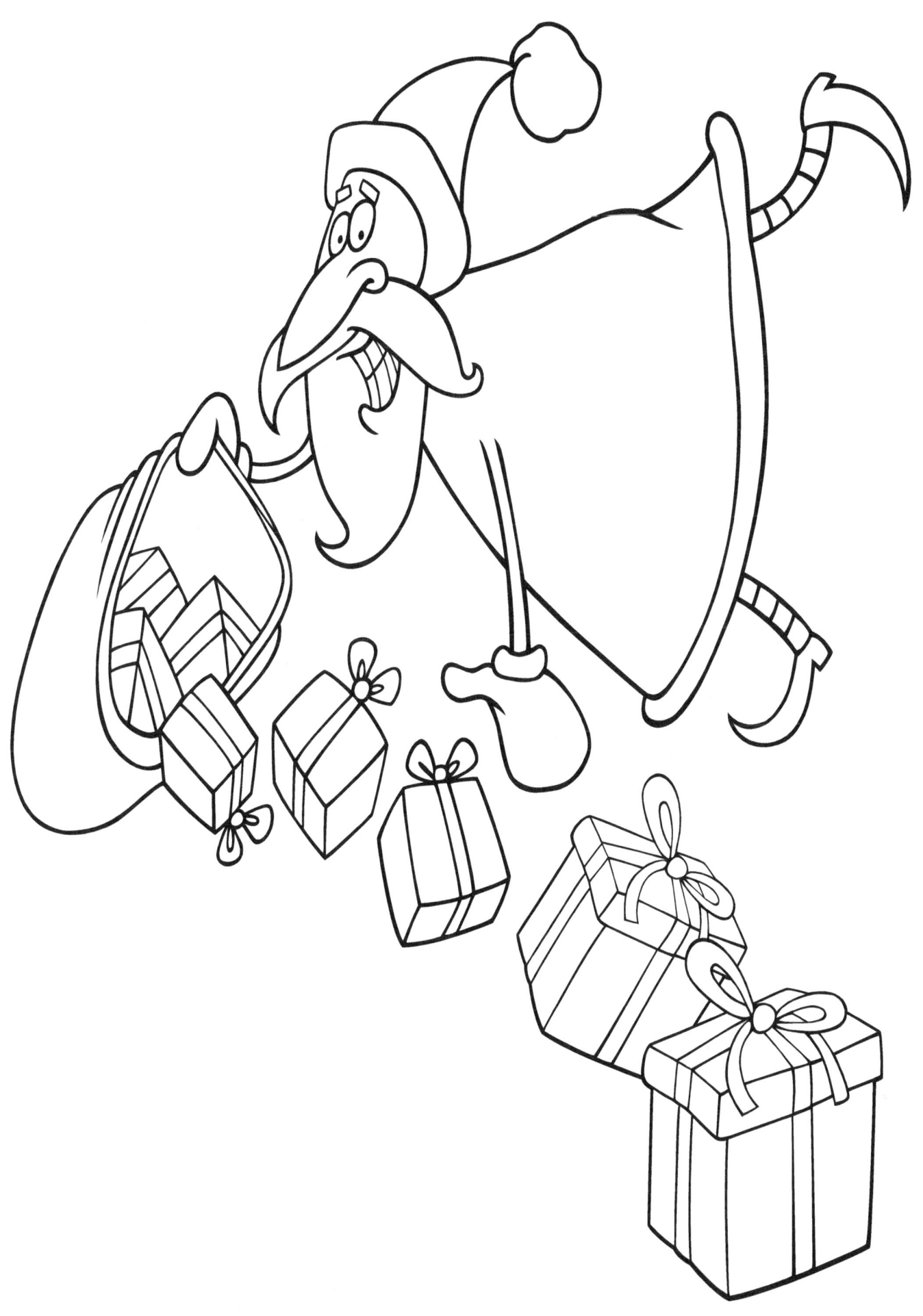

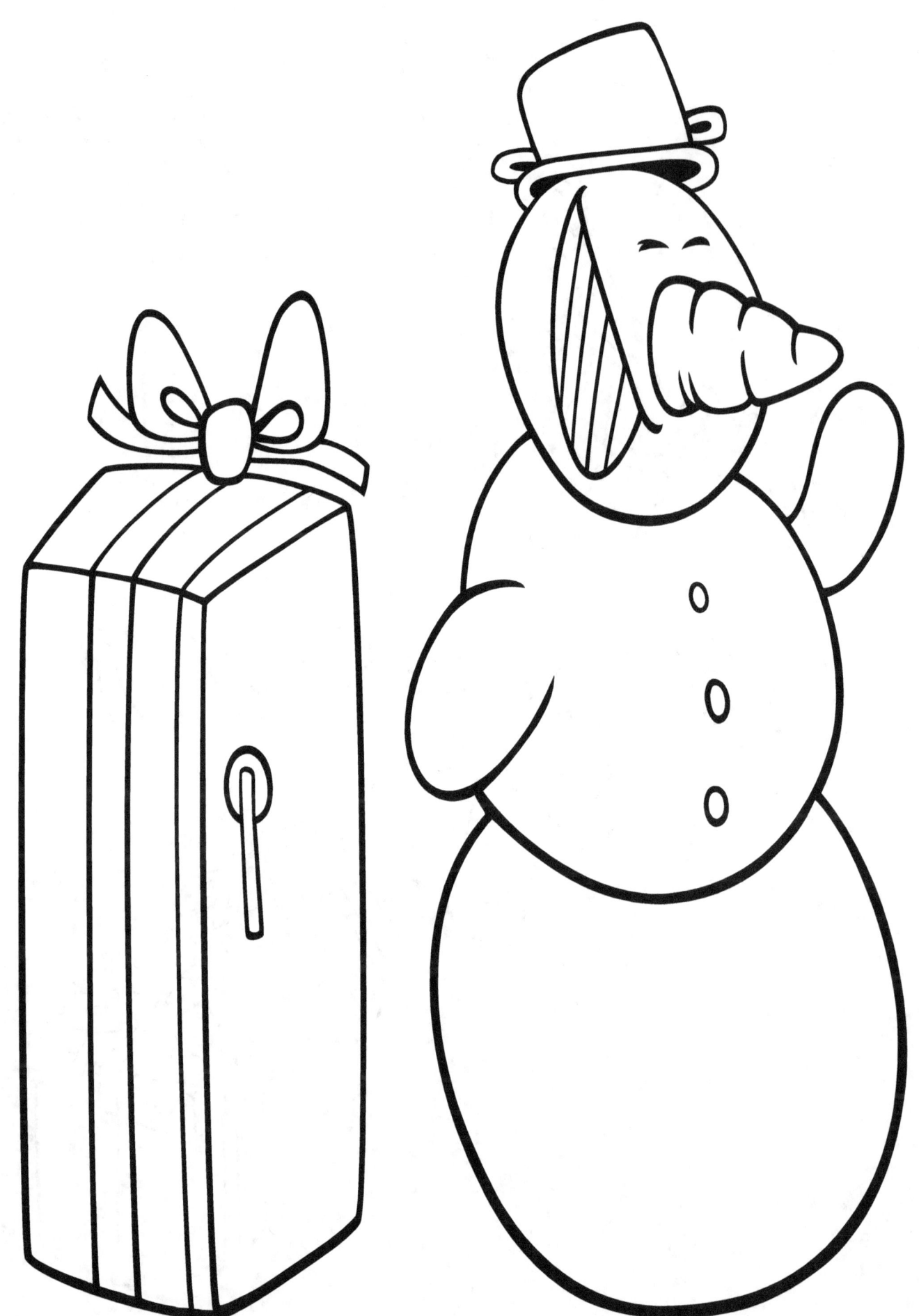

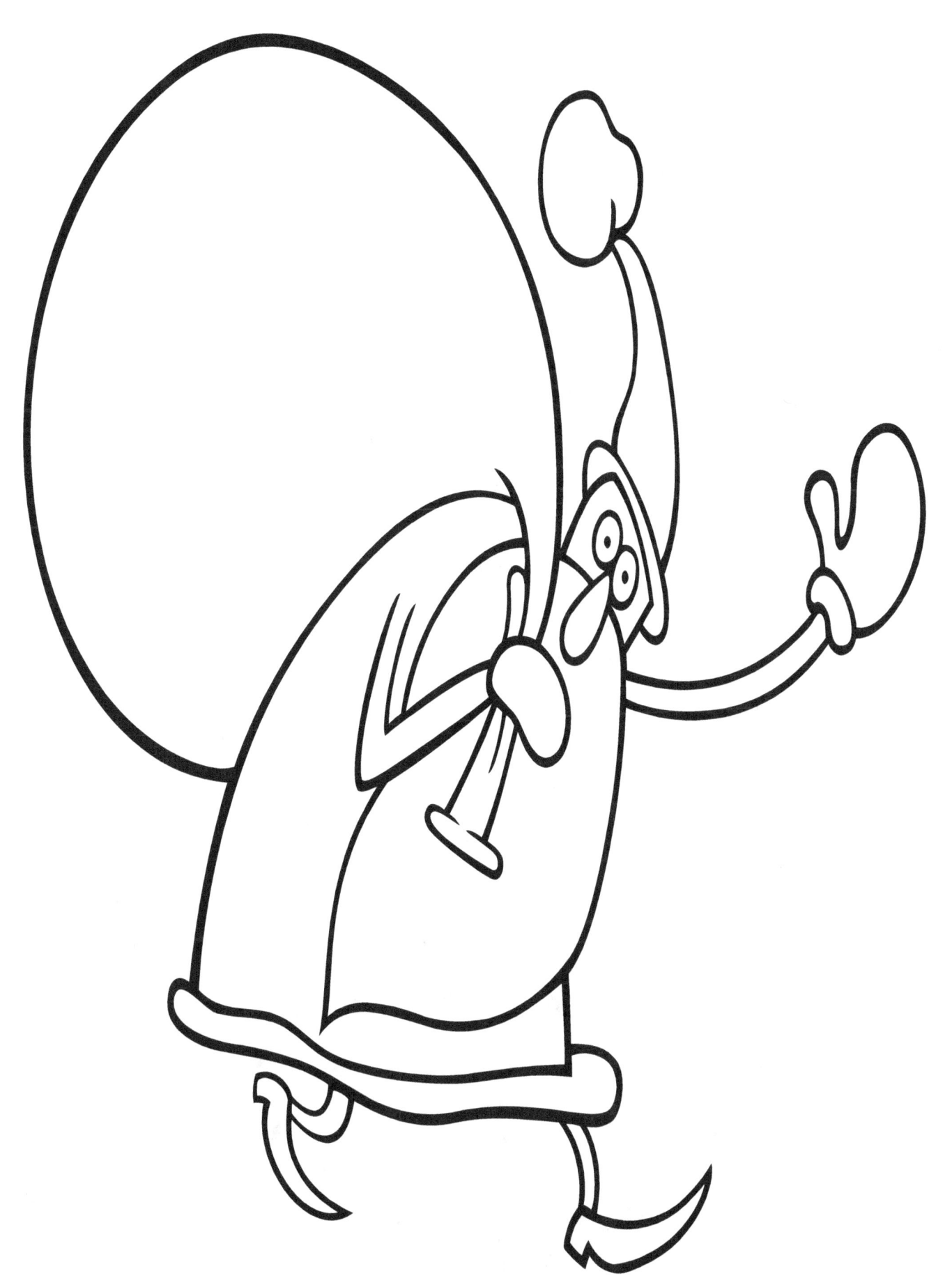

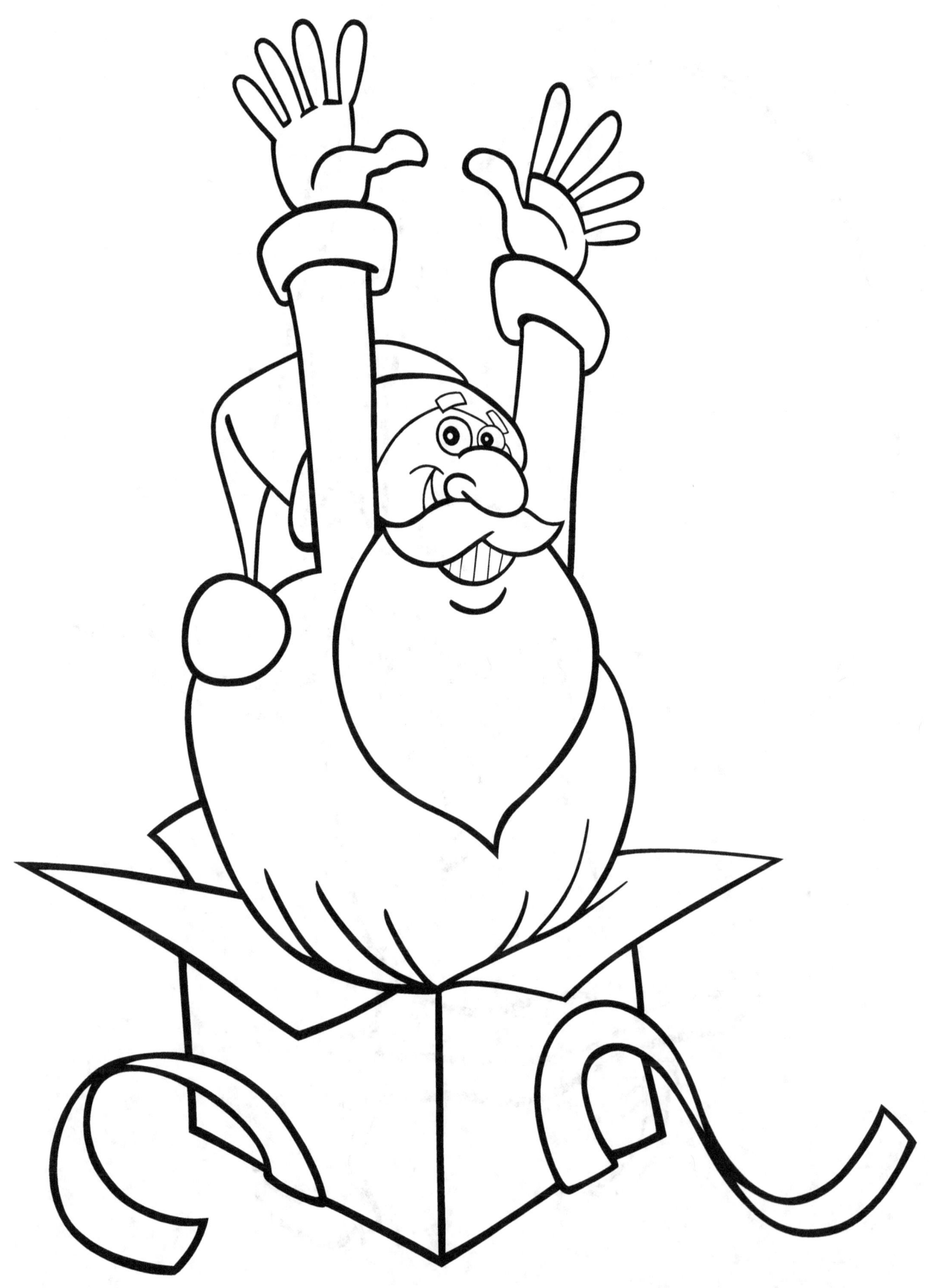

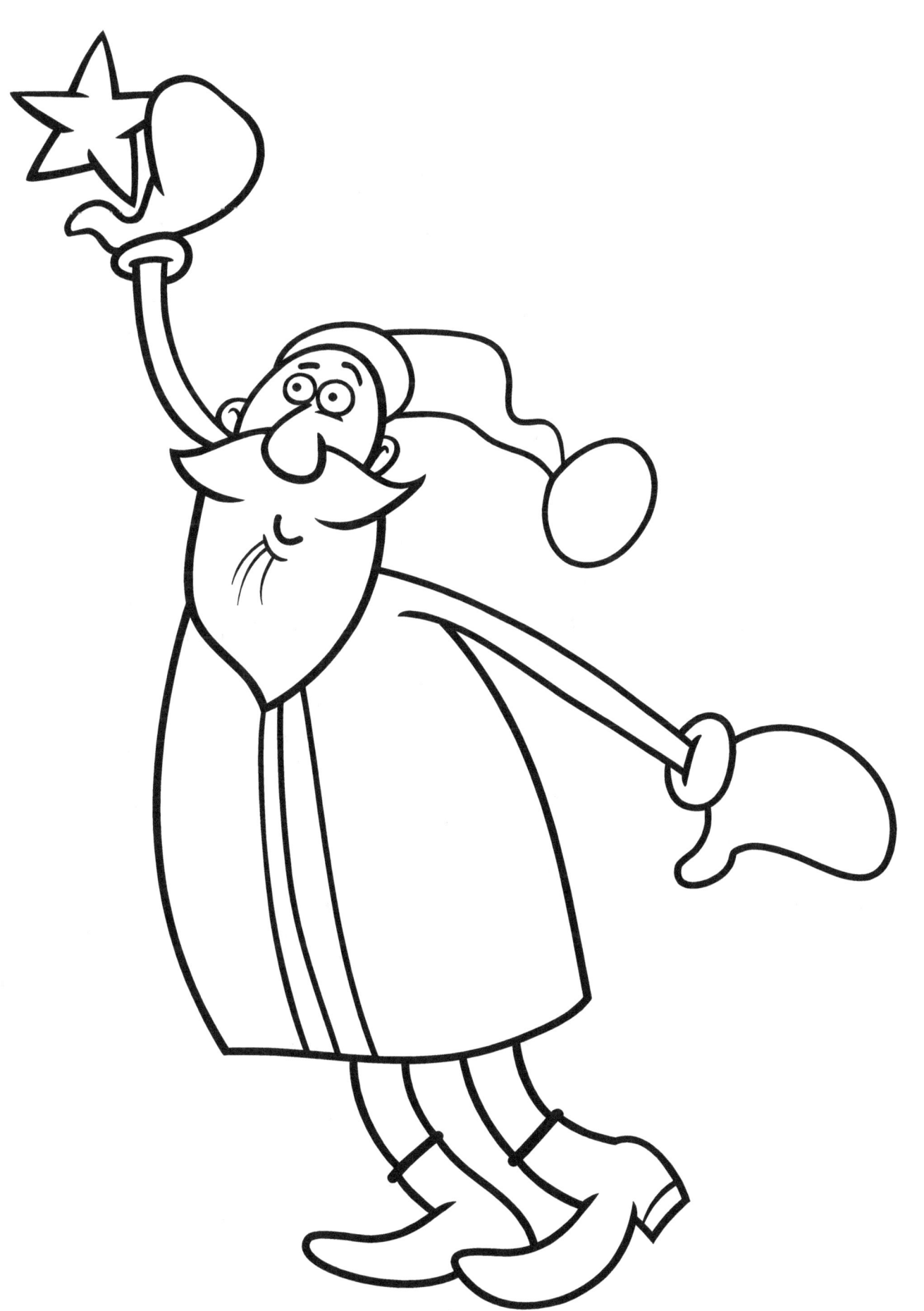

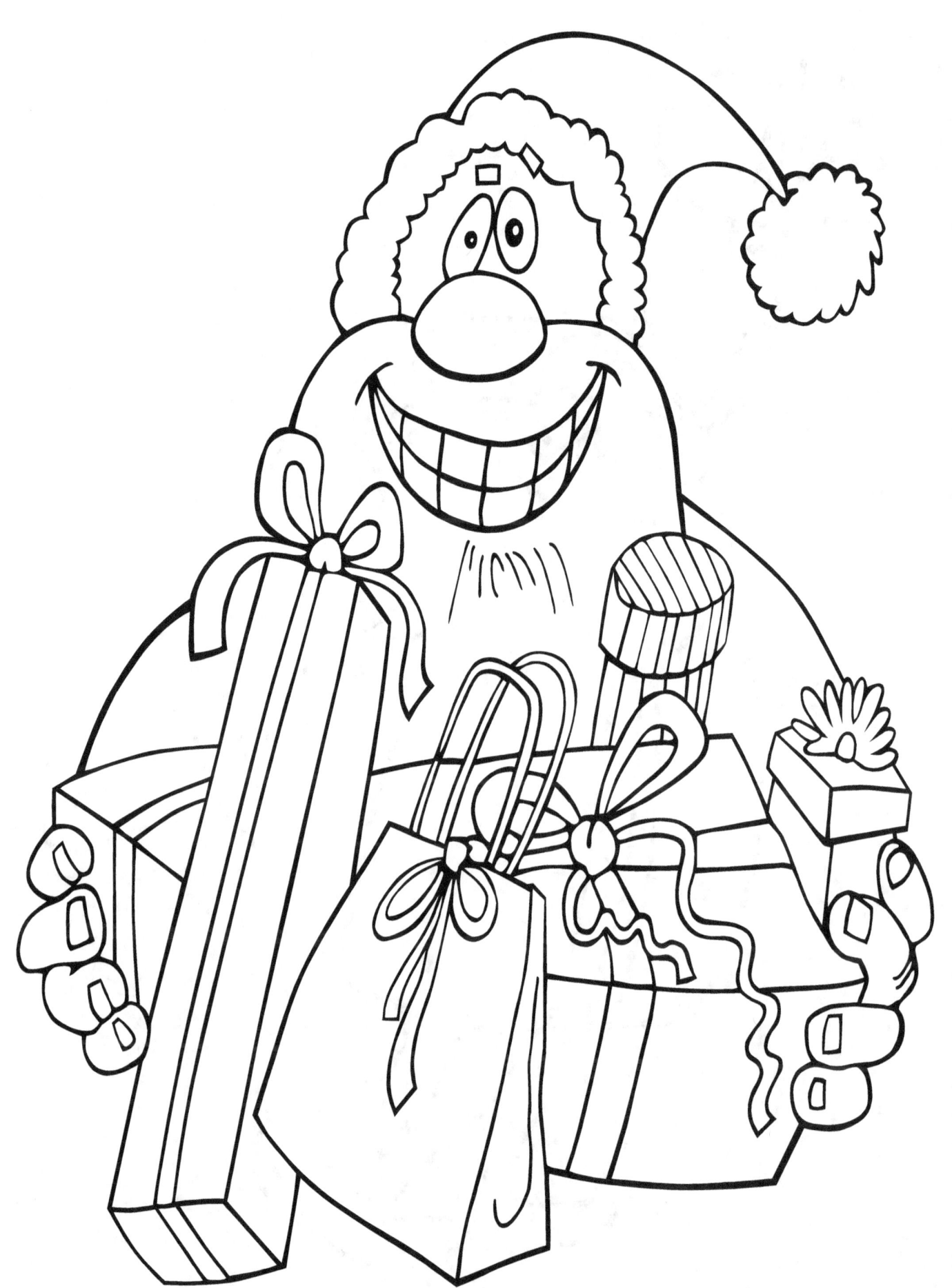

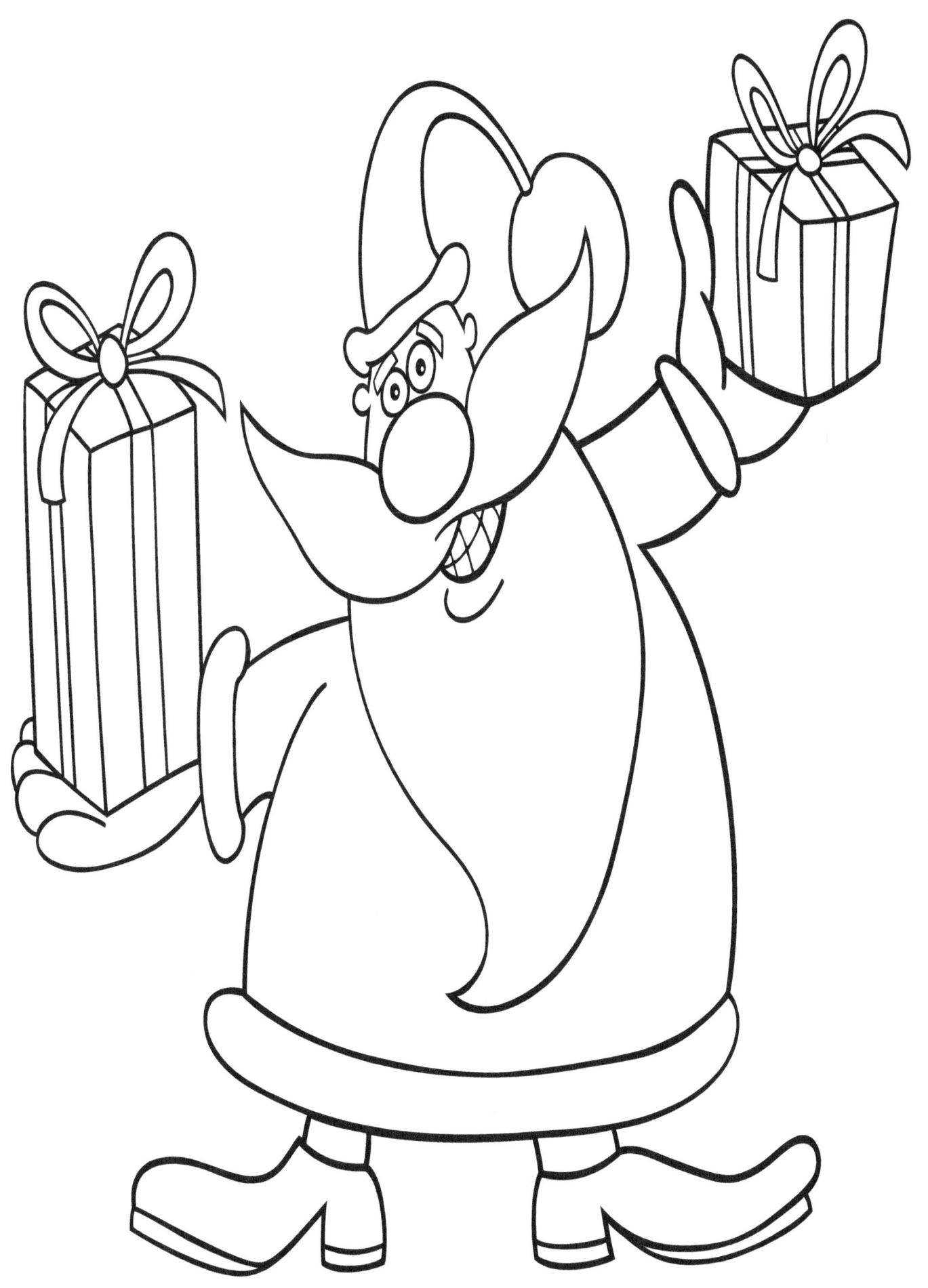

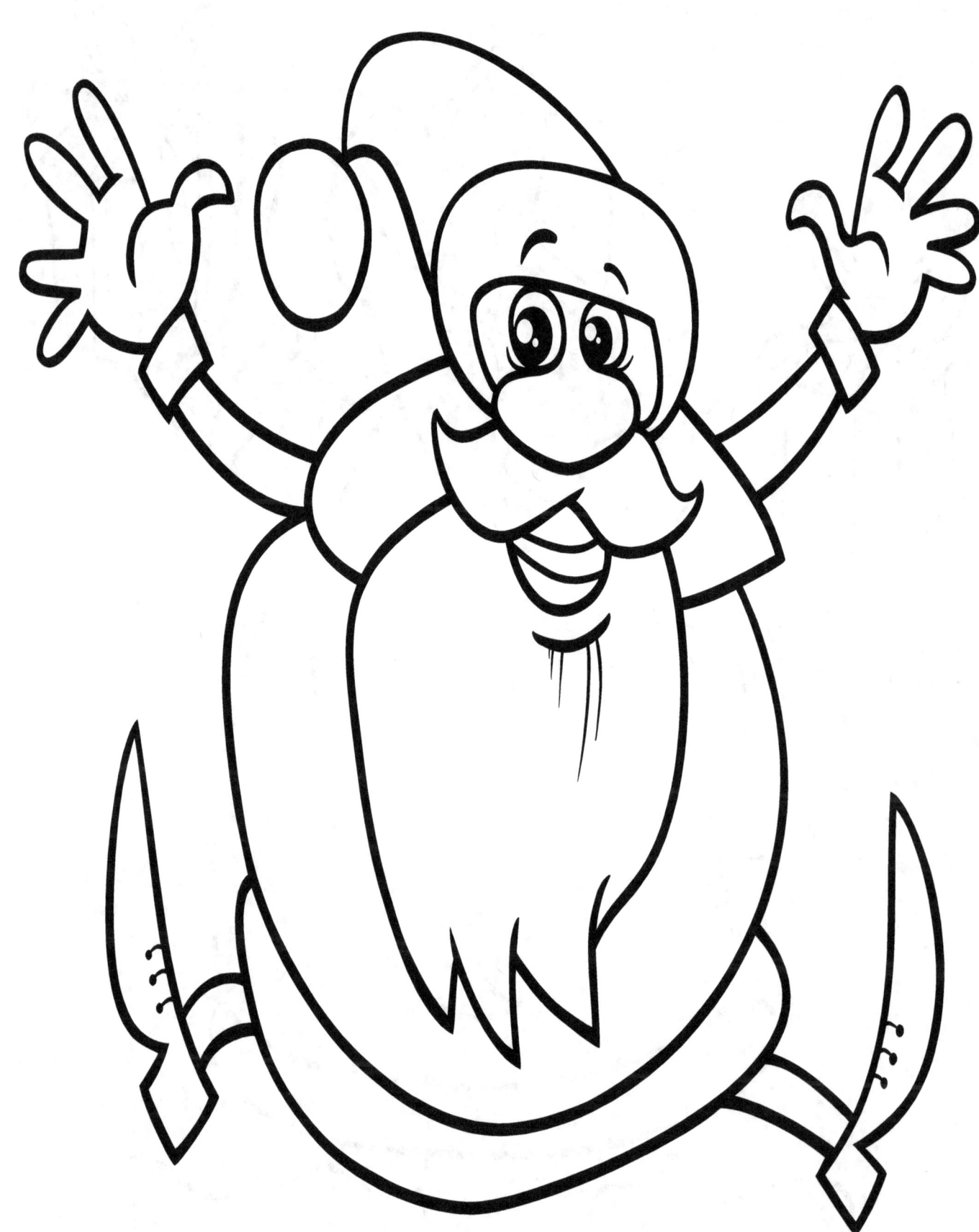

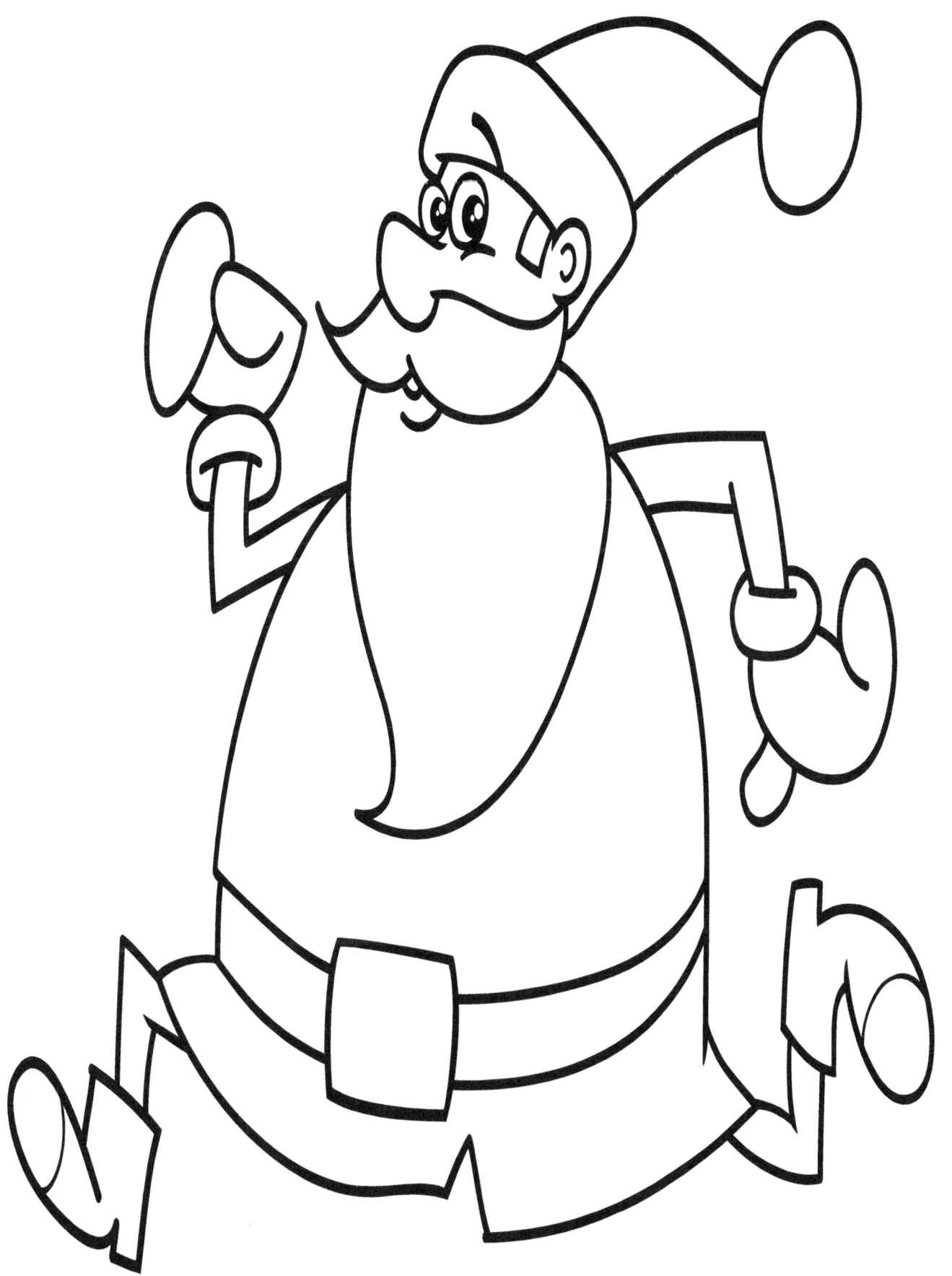

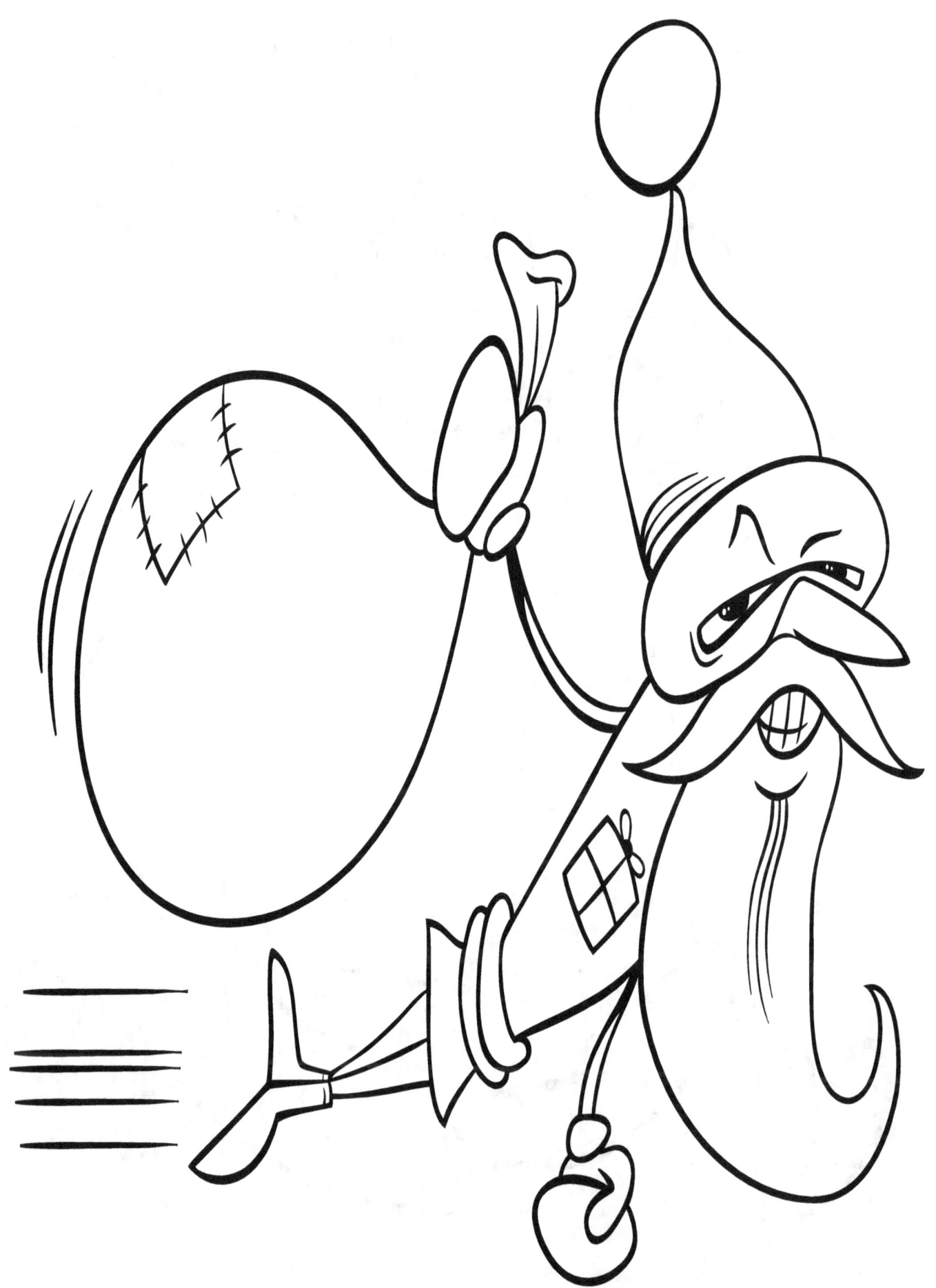

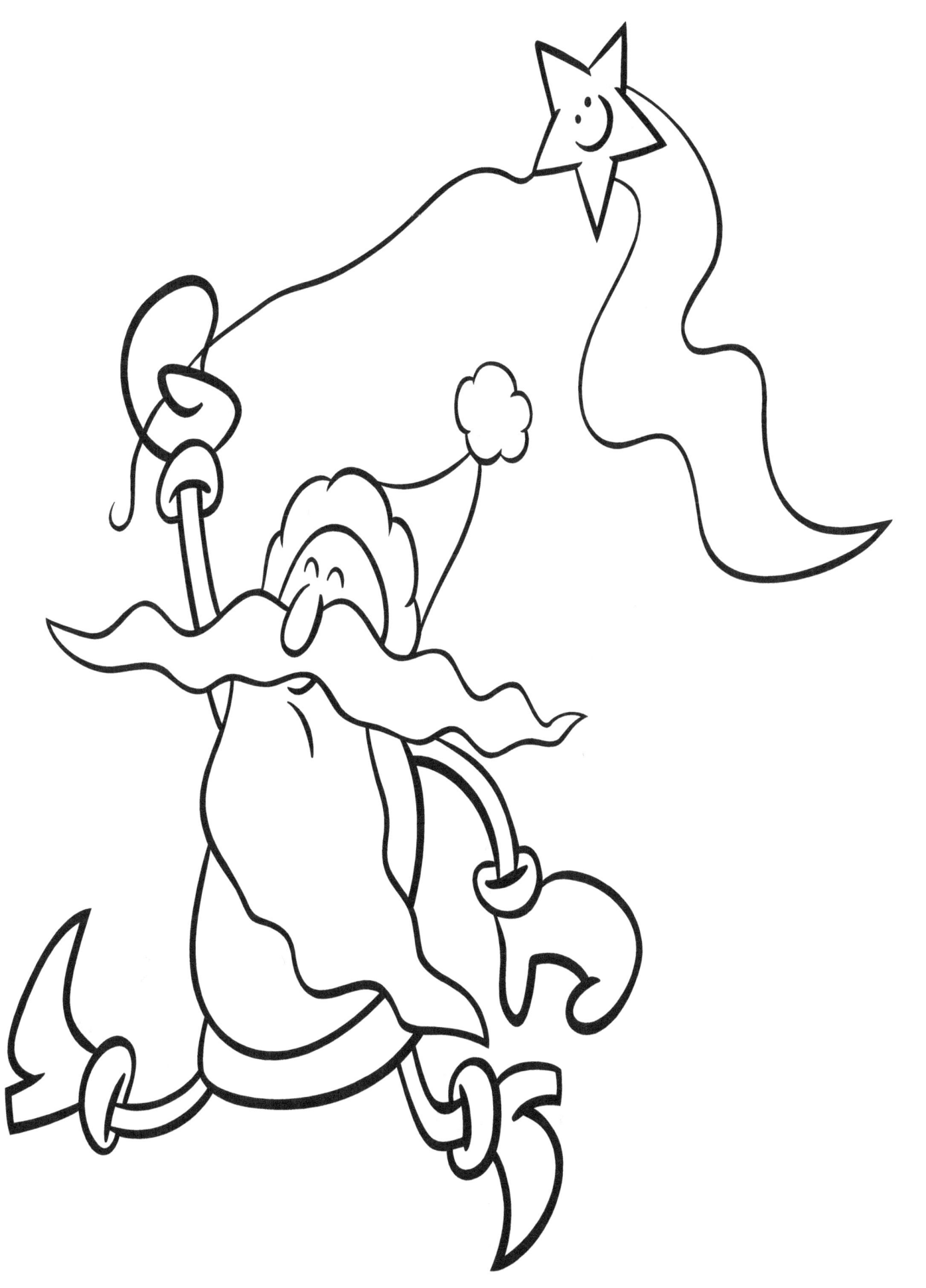

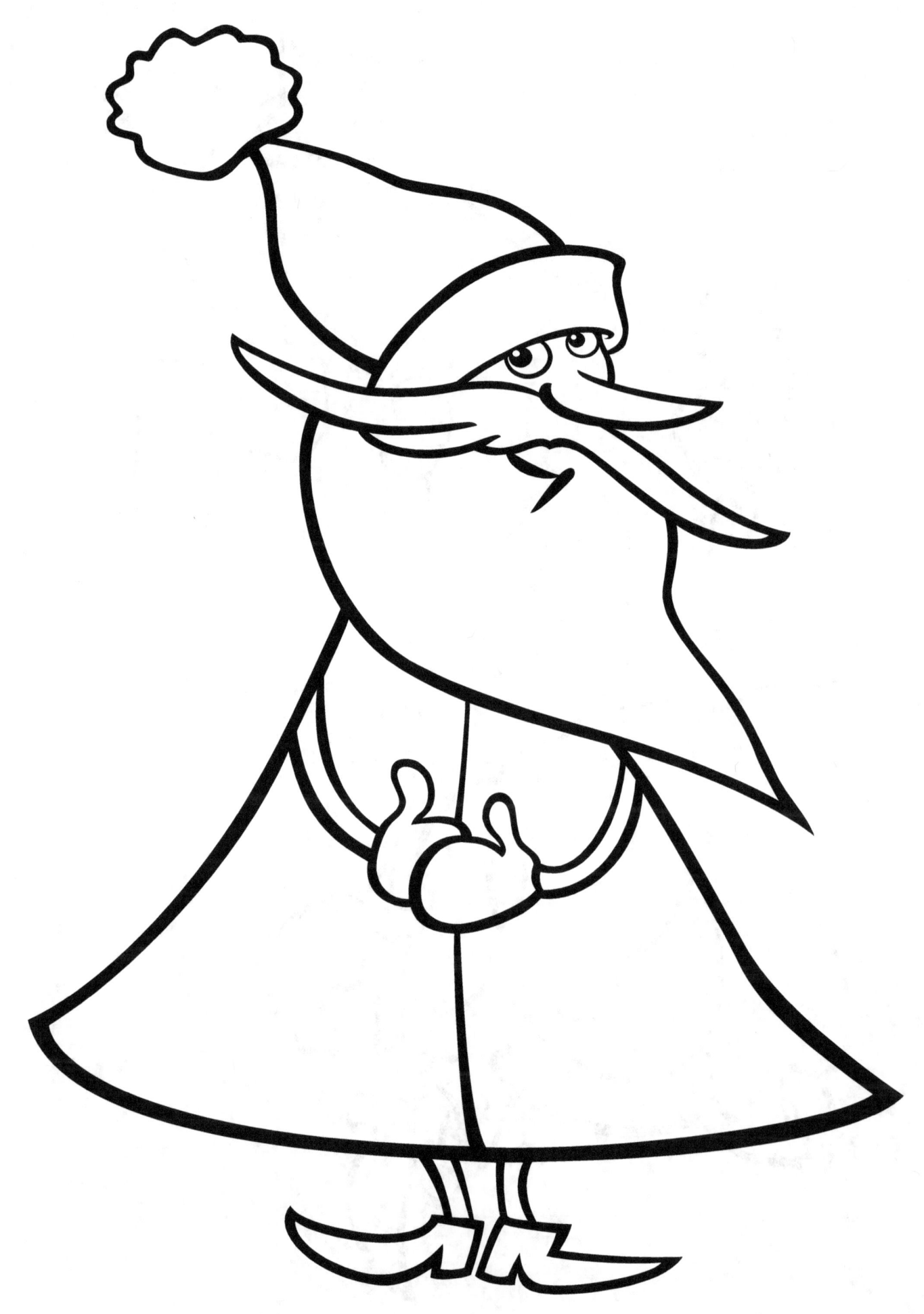

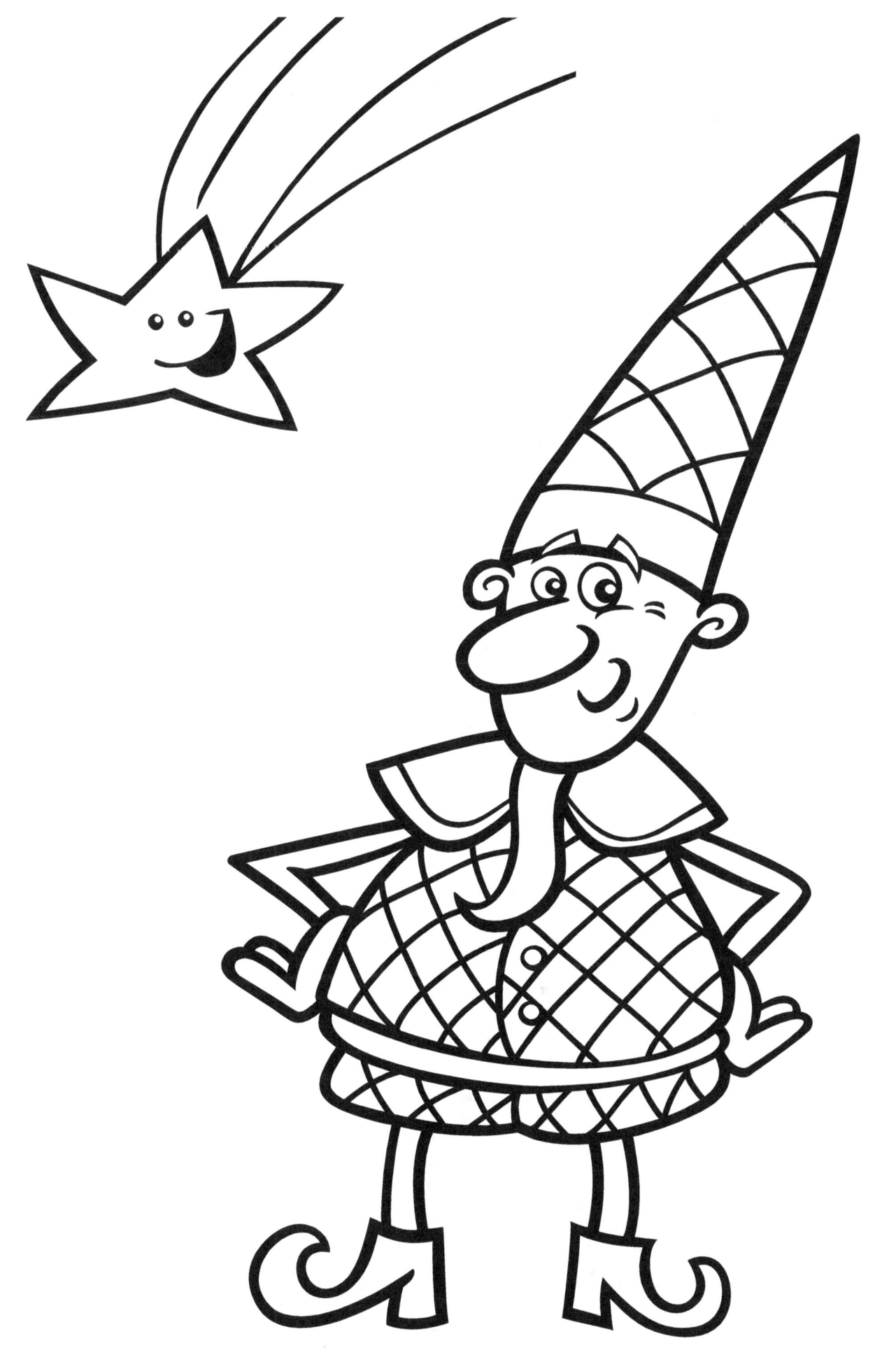

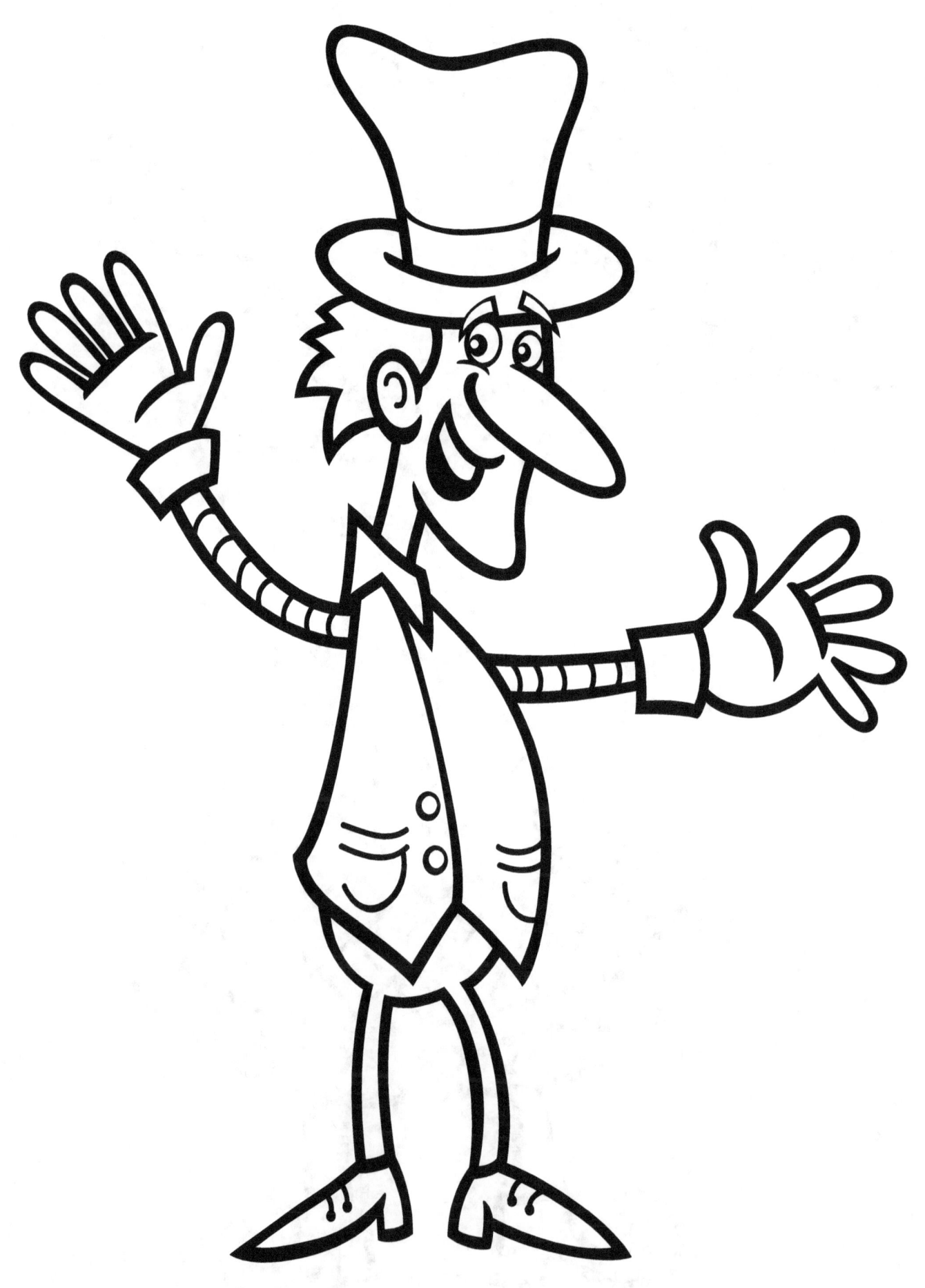

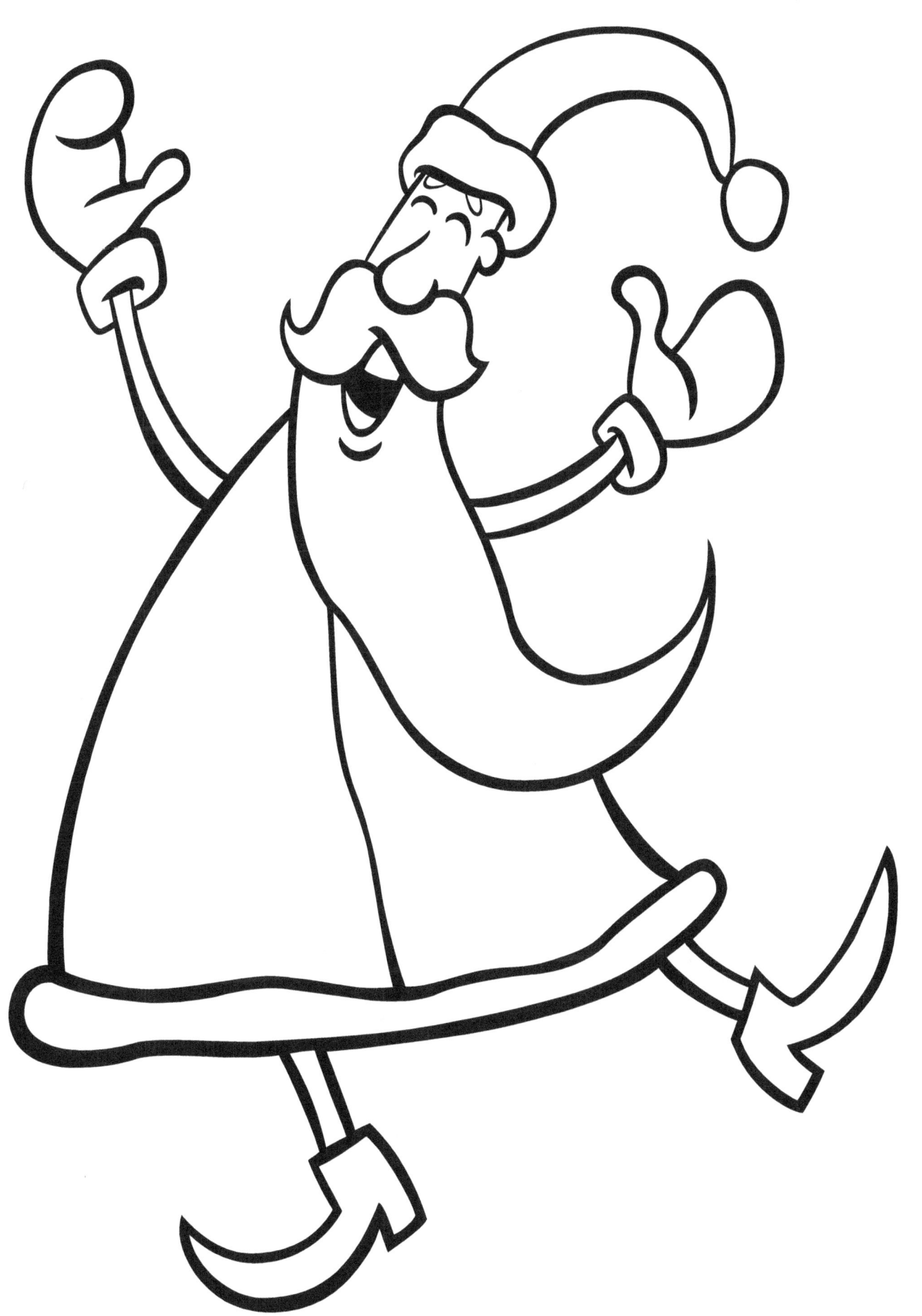

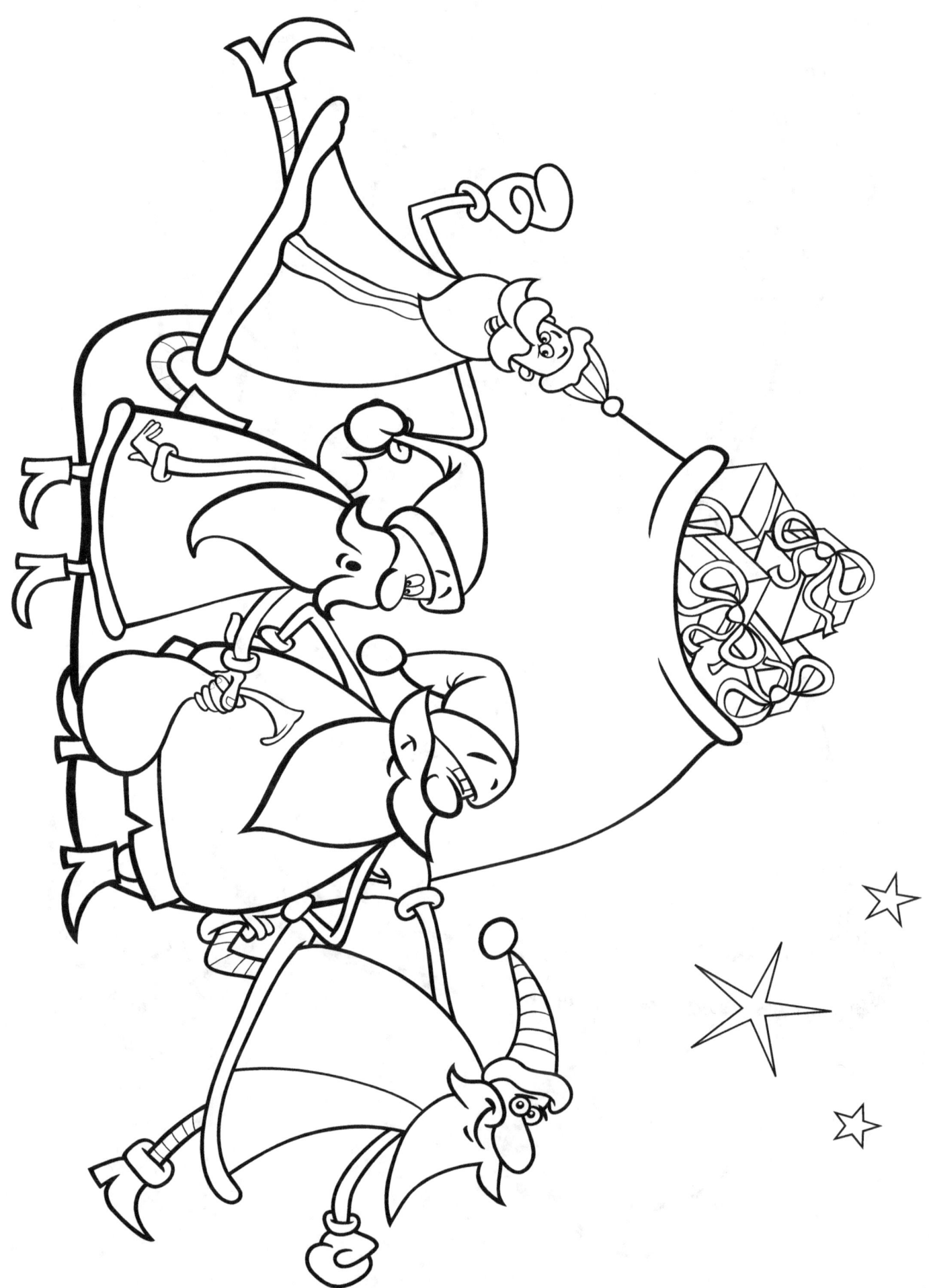

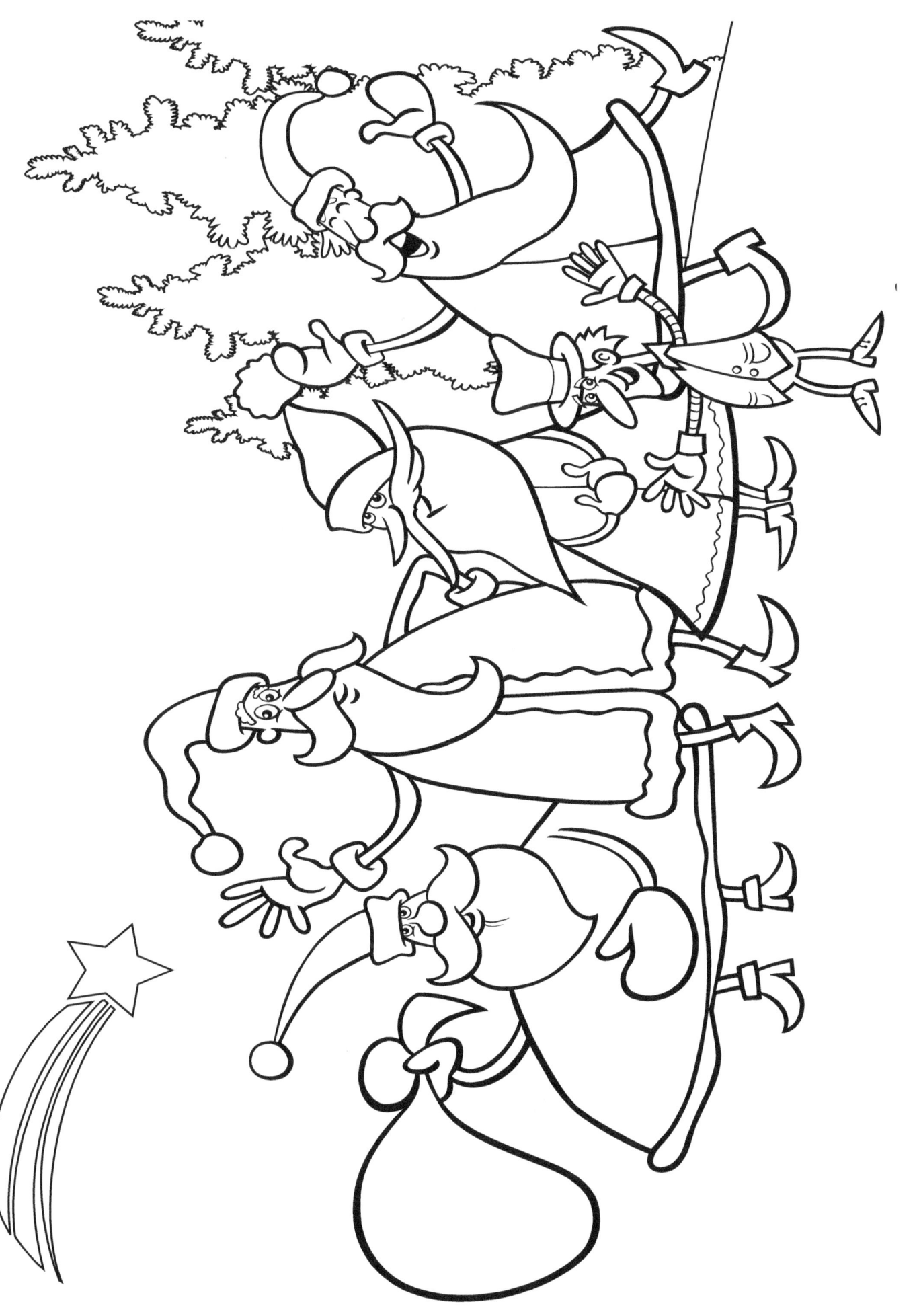

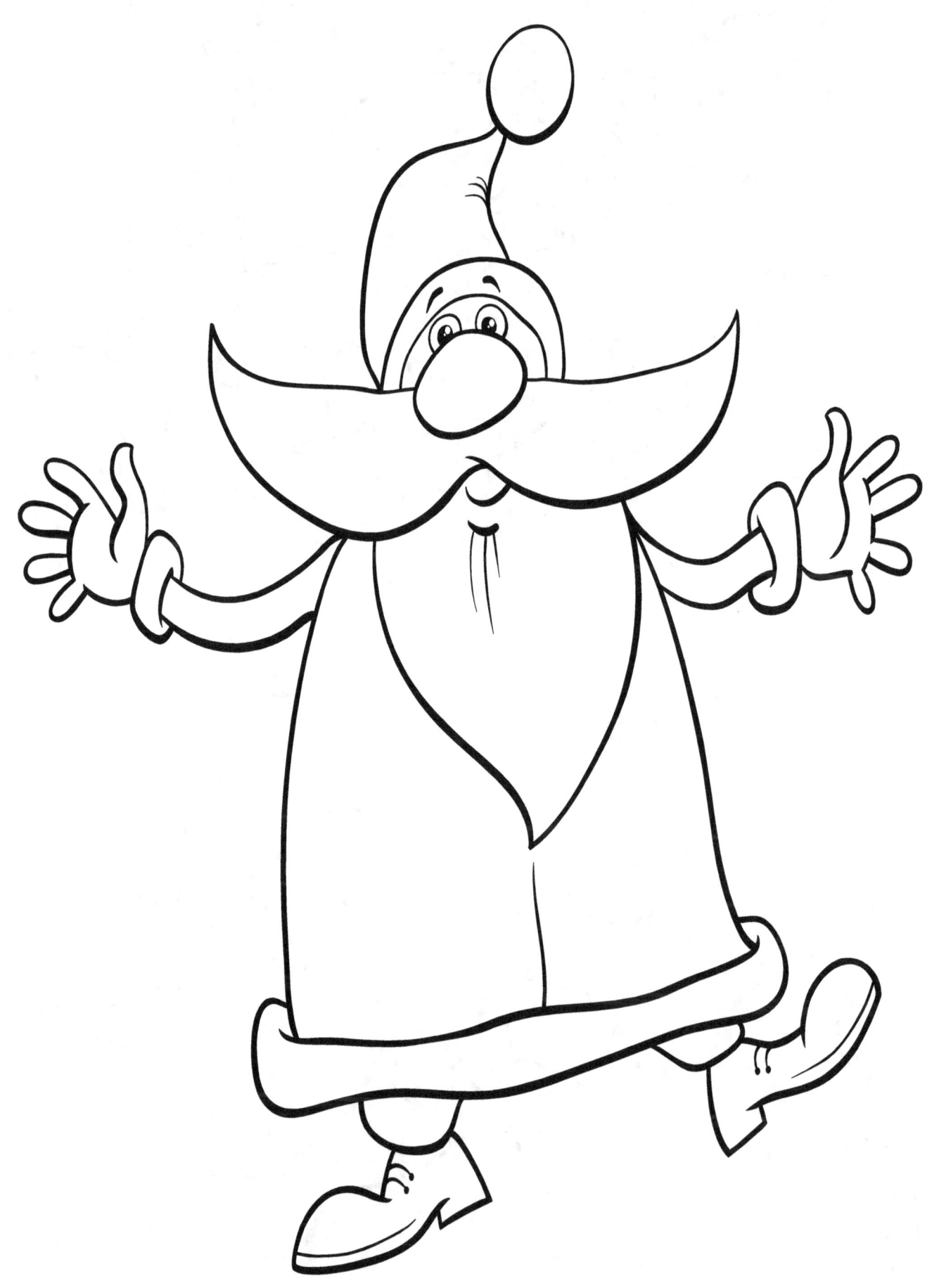

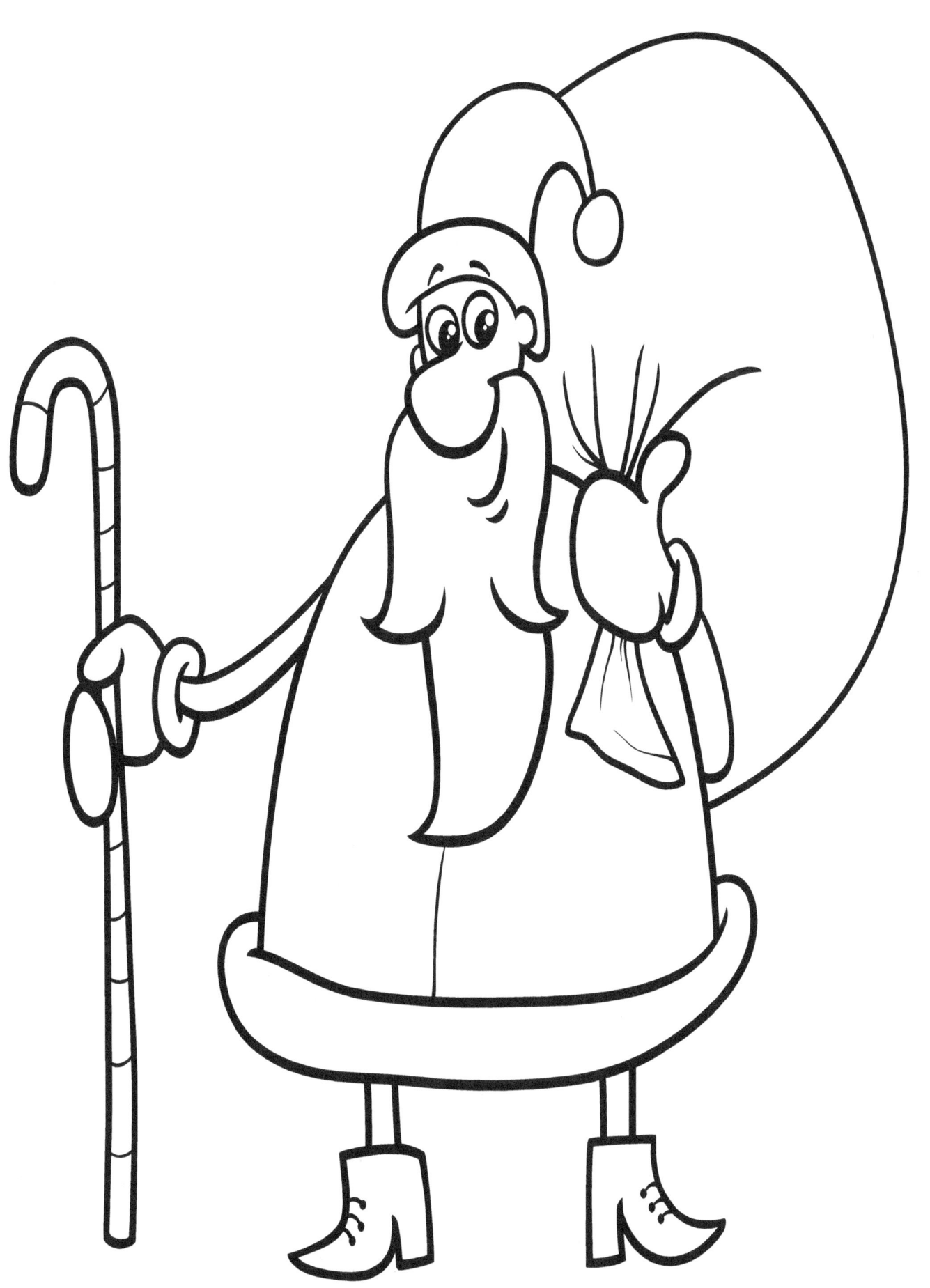

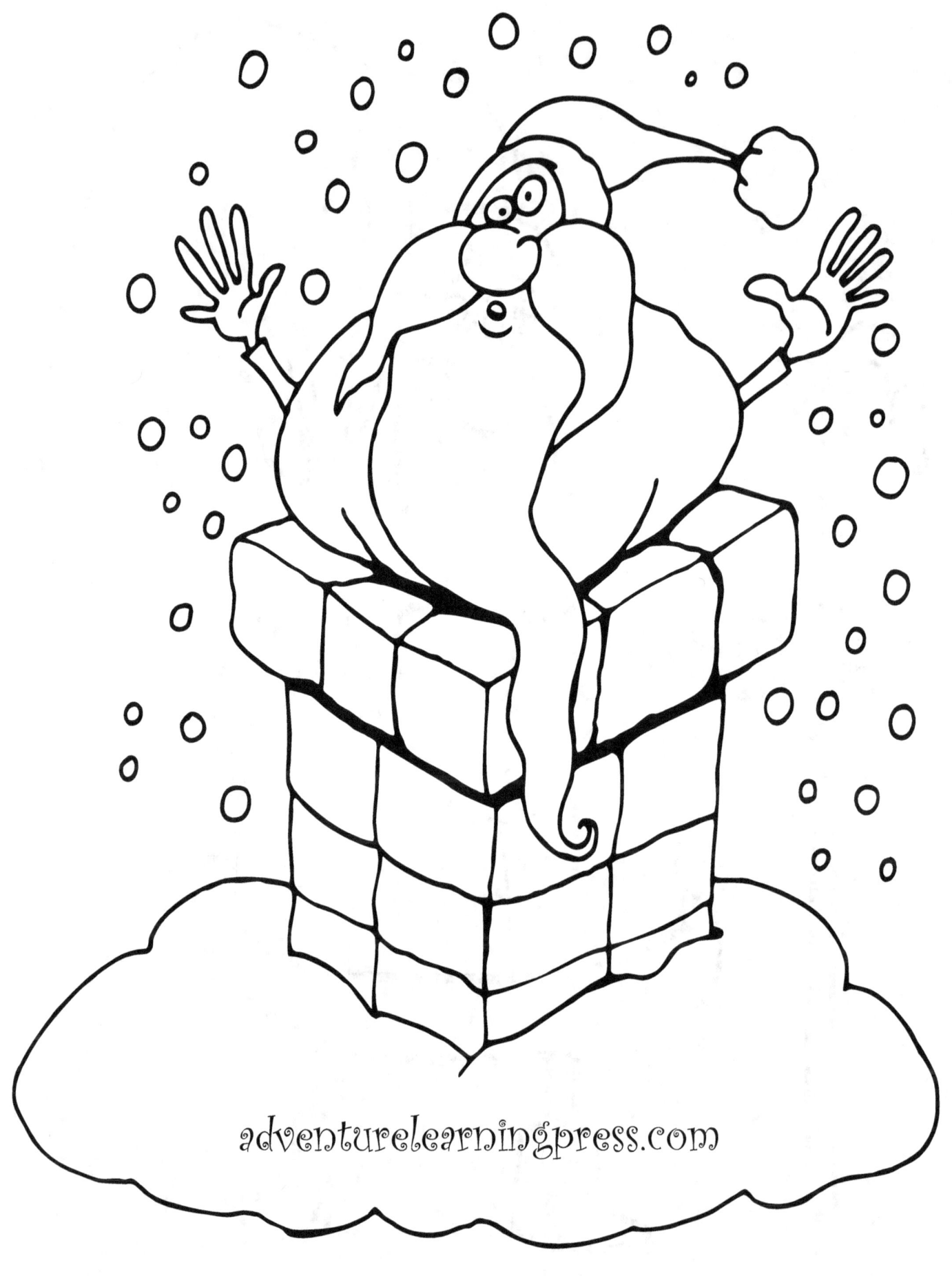

adventurelearningpress.com

www.ingramcontent.com/pod-product-compliance
Lightning Source LLC
Chambersburg PA
CBHW081808280526
45789CB00008B/3043